A

PLAN

FOR THE CONDUCT

OF

FEMALE EDUCATION,

IN

BOARDING SCHOOLS.

A

PLAN

FOR THE CONDUCT

OF

FEMALE EDUCATION,

IN

BOARDING SCHOOLS.

By ERASMUS DARWIN, M.D. F.R.S.

AUTHOR OF ZOONOMIA, AND OF THE BOTANIC GARDEN.

Delightful taſk! to watch with curious eyes
Soft forms of Thought in infant boſoms riſe,
Plant with nice hand Reflection's tender root,
And teach the young Ideas how to ſhoot!

DERBY:

PRINTED BY J. DREWRY;---FOR J. JOHNSON, ST. PAUL'S CHURCH-YARD, LONDON.

1797.

Enter'd at Stationer's Hall.

DEDICATION.

To the parents and guardians, who are solicitous about the education of their female wards, and daughters,---to the governesses of schools instituted for female tuition,---and to the teachers of young ladies in private families,---this small work is with all due respect presented

By the Author.

DERBY, *January* 1*st*, 1797.

CONTENTS.

Section

I. THE FEMALE CHARACTER.

II. MUSICK AND DANCING.

III. READING.

IV. WRITING.

V. GRAMMAR.

VI. LANGUAGES. PHYSIOGNOMY.

VII. ARITHMETIC. CARD-PLAYING.

VIII. GEOGRAPHY.

IX. HISTORY.

X. NATURAL HISTORY.

XI. RUDIMENTS OF TASTE. BEAUTY. GRACE.

XII. DRAWING AND EMBROIDERY. PERSPECTIVE.

XIII. HEATHEN MYTHOLOGY.

XIV. POLITE LITERATURE. NOVELS.

XV. ARTS AND SCIENCES.

XVI. MORALS.

XVII. COMPASSION.

XVIII. VERACITY.

XIX. PRUDENCE. JUSTICE. CHASTITY.

CONTENTS.

- XX. FORTITUDE. BASHFULNESS.
- XXI. TEMPERANCE.
- XXII. RELIGION.
- XXIII. ADDRESS.
- XXIV. CONVERSATION.
- XXV. EXERCISE. DUMB BELLS.
- XXVI. AIR. BED-ROOMS. FIRE-GRATES.
- XXVII. CARE OF THE SHAPE. COLD BATH.
- XXVIII. DRESS. EAR-RINGS. POWDER.
- XXIX. AMUSEMENTS. CHESS.
- XXX. PUNISHMENTS. REWARDS. MOTIVES.
- XXXI. LISPING.
- XXXII. STAMMERING.
- XXXIII. SQUINTING.
- XXXIV. INVOLUNTARY MOTIONS.
- XXXV. SWELL'D FINGERS, AND KIBED HEELS.
- XXXVI. BEDS. RHEUMATISM.
- XXXVII. DIET. NEW MILK.
- XXXVIII. ECONOMY.
- XXXIX. SCHOOL-EDUCATION, USES OF.
- XL. CATALOGUE OF BOOKS.
    APOLOGY FOR THE WORK.

A PLAN

FOR THE CONDUCT OF

FEMALE EDUCATION.

―――――

Section I.

THE FEMALE CHARACTER.

THE PARENTS and guardians of young ladies of the laſt half century were leſs ſolicitous about procuring for them ſo extenſive an education, as modern refinement requires. Hence it happens, that female education has not yet been reduced to a perfect ſyſtem; but is frequently directed by thoſe, who have not themſelves had a good education, or who have not ſtudied the ſubject with ſufficient attention. And tho' many ingenious remarks are to be found in the works of Locke, Rouſſeau, Genlis,

Genlis, and other writers still more modern; yet few of them are exactly applicable to the management of boarding schools; the improvement of which is the intent of the present treatise.

The advantages of a good education consist in uniting health and agility of body with chearfulness and activity of mind; in superadding graceful movements to the former, and agreeable tastes to the latter; and in the acquirement of the rudiments of such arts and sciences, as may amuse ourselves, or gain us the esteem of others; with a strict attention to the culture of morality and religion.

The female character should possess the mild and retiring virtues rather than the bold and dazzling ones; great eminence in almost any thing is sometimes injurious to a young lady; whose temper and disposition should appear to be pliant rather than robust; to be ready to take impressions rather than to be decidedly mark'd; as great apparent strength of character, however excellent, is liable to alarm both her own and the other sex; and to create admiration rather than affection.

There are however situations in single life; in which, after the completion of their school-education, ladies may cultivate to

any

any extent the fine arts or the sciences for their amusement or instruction. And there are situations in a married state; which may call forth all the energies of the mind in the care, education, or provision, for a family; which the inactivity, folly, or death of a husband may render necessary. Hence if to softness of manners, complacency of countenance, gentle unhurried motion, with a voice clear and yet tender, the charms which enchant all hearts! can be superadded internal strength and activity of mind, capable to transact the business or combat the evils of life; with a due sense of moral and religious obligation; all is obtain'd, which education can supply; the female character becomes compleat, excites our love, and commands our admiration.

Education should draw the outline, and teach the use of the pencil; but the exertions of the individual must afterwards introduce the various gradations of shade and colour, must illuminate the landscape, and fill it with the beautiful figures of the Graces and the Virtues.

Section II.

MUSICK AND DANCING

ARE generally taught by masters, who profess those arts; concerning which we shall only observe, that they are frequently believed to be of too great importance in female education; and on that account that too much time is expended on their acquirement. It is perhaps more desirable, that young ladies should play, sing, and dance, only so well as to amuse themselves and their friends, than to practise those arts in so eminent a degree as to astonish the public; because a great apparent attention to trivial accomplishments is liable to give a suspicion, that more valuable acquisitions have been neglected. And, as they consist in an exhibition of the person, they are liable to be attended with vanity, and to extinguish the blush of youthful timidity; which is in young ladies the most powerful of their exterior charms.

Such masters should be chosen to instruct young ladies in these accomplishments, as are not only well qualified to sing and play, or to dance themselves; but also who can teach with good temper and genteel behaviour: they should recollect, that vulgar manners, with the sharp gestures of anger, and its disagreeable tones of voice, are unpardonable in those, who profess to teach graceful motion, and melodious expression; and may affect the taste and temper of their pupils, so as to be more injurious to their education; than any thing, which they are able to teach them, can counterbalance.

Section III.

READING.

As Reading is as much a language to the eye, as speaking is to the ear; it requires much time and labour for children to acquire both these languages. Such books should therefore be put into their hands, as join amusement with instruction, and thus lighten the fatigue of continued application, as Sandford and Merton, Parent's assistant, Evenings at home, and many others.

SECT. 3. READING.

In learning to read aloud, a clear and distinct enunciation is seldom acquired at schools; which is owing to the child standing close to the teacher, who looks over the book along with it; and hence the pupil finds no difficulty in being understood, even when she pronounces only half words. This however is easily remedied by placing the reader at the distance of two yards or more from the hearer; then the young scholar soon finds, that she is not understood, unless she expresses herself with clear articulation. For this purpose the teacher should always be provided with a duplicate of the book, she teaches; that she may not be necessitated to look over the shoulder of her pupil.

As the young scholars advance in the knowledge of language, other books must be taught them both in prose and poetry; such as may improve their minds in the knowledge of things, in morality, religion, or which may form their taste. A great number of books for the use of children has been published in late years; many of them by very ingenious writers, and well adapted to the purpose designed, of such of these, as have come to my knowledge, a catalogue shall be given at the end of this treatise.

Section IV.

WRITING.

WRITING, as it keeps the body in a fix'd posture, as well as drawing, and needlework, should not be too long applied to at a time; since the body, and even the countenance, may thus get a certain tendency to one attitude; as is seen in children, who are brought up to some mechanic art, as in polishing buttons or precious stones on a lathe. A proper manner of holding the pen, or pencil, or needle, with an easy but graceful attitude of the person, and an agreeable moderate attention of the countenance, should first be taught; for which purposes an inclined desk has many advantages over an horizontal table for the books, or working frames; as the body is thence less bent forwards; and the light in general situations more vividly reflected to the eye.

If the desk be sixteen inches broad, the furthermost edge of it should rise about three inches and half from the horizontal line;

which

which produces the moſt convenient inclination, and the table or frame, which ſupports it, for the uſe of the taller children, ſhould riſe about two feet eight inches from the ground.

Section v.

GRAMMAR,

WHICH is an abſtract ſcience teaching the texture of language, is too hard for very young minds; and is therefore generally taught too early: and the ſame may be ſaid of Arithmetic. The Engliſh grammars in general uſe at ſchools are both tedious and defective compoſitions; an epitome, or extract, from Lowth's grammar, with the late improvements of Mr. Horne Tooke in the theory of language, would well ſupply this branch of knowledge; and might be given to the public under the name of a "rational Engliſh grammar."

Mrs. Devis has publiſh'd a ſmall and uſeful rudiment of grammar purpoſely for the uſe of young ladies; which may be taught as an introduction to Lowth's grammar. The Abbé Gaultier's

Jeu de Grammaire may perhaps be render'd amusing to children, and convey to them ideas of the French grammar. It is sold by Elmsley in the Strand, and by Mrs. Harrow in Pall-Mall; but is perhaps better adapted to private families, than to schools.

Section VI.

LANGUAGES.

THE necessity of learning some antient or foreign languages imposes a laborious task on the youth of both sexes; which consumes years of their precious time, which might otherwise be employed in the acquisition of sciences. The difficulty of obtaining a competent knowledge of the Greek or Latin language is many times greater than that of obtaining any modern one; as may be deduced from the innumerable changes of the termination of their nouns, adjectives, and verbs; which to a beginner are all so many new words. And as the works of the best writers in these languages have been translated into our own, it is less necessary in the education of ladies to expend so much time and labour in acquiring them. But as the French and Italian are less difficult to learn, and contain new books of taste and knowledge, which are yearly publish'd in this age of literature; and as they are convenient for conversing with foreigners, who come hither, or in our travelling into other countries; and lastly, as they are agreeable as well as fashionable studies; the pupils of boarding schools should be encouraged to attain one or both of them.

The method recommended by Mr. Locke in his treatise on education, sect. 162, of teaching languages by conversation, will on trial be generally found successful in respect to modern languages with even the youngest children. Nevertheless a knowledge of grammar should afterwards be taught with care, if the child be too young at first to attend to it; for without the aid of grammar not only the French or Italian languages, but even the English will not always be spoken or written with perfect accuracy.

For this purpose of acquiring modern languages by conversation, a school generally supplies better opportunities than a private family, besides the advantage of some degree of emulation, which frequently exists, where children converse together: another advantage of infantine society is, that they learn many other things, as well as languages, by repeating them to each other; and obtain,

obtain, what is seldom to be acquired from adult companions, some knowledge of physiognomy; as the passions of children are more legibly express'd on their countenances than at a maturer age. This knowledge of physiognomy, which is perhaps only to be acquired at schools, by giving a promptitude of understanding the present approbation or dislike, and the good or bad designs, of those whom we converse with, becomes of hourly use in almost every department of life.

Section VII.

ARITHMETIC

LIKE grammar is an abstract science, which is frequently attempted to be taught too early; at the same time it may be observed, that the early initiation of most children into card playing before they come to school, by giving clear and visible ideas of the ten first numerals, seems greatly to facilitate their acquirement of arithmetic; and if this fashionable amusement could be so managed by the parents, who allow it to their children, as not to excite a desire of gain along with a contest of ingenuity, it might

might be rendered, in some measure, advantageous by exciting the mind to activity in this branch of science; but is nevertheless not proper to be used in schools, where it's effects on the passions cannot be sufficiently watched, and counteracted.

So much of the science of numbers as is in common use, as the numeration, subtraction, multiplication, and division of money, should be learnt with accuracy; to which should be added the rule of three, and decimal fractions; which will abundantly repay the labour of acquiring them by the pleasure and utility, which will perpetually result from the knowledge of them thro' life. The higher parts of arithmetic, as algebra and fluxions, belong to the abstruser sciences.

There are many introductory books to the science of arithmetic; those I have heard most recommended are Vise's tutor's guide, Hutton's practical arithmetic, and Wingate's arithmetic; but it is probable, that most of the introductory treatises to arithmetic must be nearly of equal excellence.

Section VIII.

GEOGRAPHY.

So much of this science, as depends only on memory, may be taught to children in their early years. They should be taught to point out on large maps the counties of England, and then the principal divisions of Europe, and of the other quarters of the world; and lastly to trace out the principal rivers and mountains, which ingrave or imboss it's surface, which is much to be prefer'd to dissected maps; as it is the situations, rather than the exact forms of counties and of countries, which should be attended to. Afterwards the use of the globes should be explain'd; and some short outline of astronomy ought to accompany these lectures.

A compendious system of geography on cards, published by Mr. Newberry, in St. Paul's church yard, supplies a very convenient method of instructing children. Other geographical cards by Bowles, tho' they only mention the latitude and longitude of important

important places, may also be used with advantage. The maps publish'd by Mr. Faden, which have blank outlines to be filled up by the student, are well designed, and not very expensive. The Abbé Gualtier's cours de Geographie form'd into a game may, like his game at grammar, be render'd amusing to children, and are tolerably well adapted both to private families, where there are but few pupils, and to public seminaries of instruction.

Fairman's geography, a small octavo sold by Johnson, contains a short account of the planets, and use of the globes. Brooks's gazetteer is an useful work; and some other good geographical publications are mentioned in the catalogue of books at the end of this work.

Section IX.

HISTORY.

THE history of mankind is connected with the knowledge of the earth, which they cultivate. A summary of the history of England should precede that of other nations, as it may be more interesting,

interesting, and more easily comprehended by English children. Afterwards an abridgement of the history of other nations both antient and modern may be collected from various writers, but are some of them already made concise and agreeable by Dr. Goldsmith in his histories of Greece and Rome, as well as of England and Scotland; which however cannot be well remembered without a previous knowledge of geography, or by consulting maps with every change of place in the account of transactions.

Afterwards a brief, but correct knowledge of history still more ancient, and of chronology, comprehending the four great empires of the world, with the rise of the present kingdoms of Europe from the fall of the last, may be acquired according to the plan of Mrs. Chapone in her letters on the improvement of the mind. This outline of history and chronology may be readily and agreeably learned from Priestley's chart of history; which with his chart of biography should hang amongst a collection of large well-colour'd maps in the parlour of a boarding school, that they may frequently encounter the eyes of the young students.

Section X.

NATURAL HISTORY.

THE history of the various other animals is also connected with our knowledge of the various parts of the earth, which they inhabit. This is termed natural history, and may be taught to children earlier than the histories of mankind, as being easier to their comprehensions, and thence more interesting and agreeable to them. Dr. Goldsmith in his history of animated nature has also made this part of knowledge of easy access; and Mr. Bewick's account of quadrupedes, with wood-prints of the animals, and amusing tale-pieces to the sections, are quite charming to children. To these should be added a treatise on birds, with the scientific names admirably adapted for the use of schools by Mr. Galton, publish'd by Johnson in St. Paul's church yard, London, in three small volumes. And besides these, children should be permitted occasionally to inspect the collections of foreign animals, which are frequently exhibited in this country;

as an examination of the objects themselves conveys clearer ideas than prints and descriptions, and at the same time adds to their knowledge, and gratifies their curiosity.

Section XI.

THE RUDIMENTS OF TASTE

ARE too much neglected in most boarding schools; these should be taught with some care, as perhaps peculiarly belonging to Ladies; since taste enters into their dress, their motions, their manners, as well as into all the fine arts, which they have leisure to cultivate; as drawing, painting, modelling, making artificial flowers, embroidery; writing letters, reading, speaking, and into almost every circumstance of life.

The general rudiments of taste are to be acquired first by reading books, which treat professedly on the subject; as the ten papers by Mr. Addison on the power of imagination in the Spectator, vol. 6, No. 411; Akinside's pleasures of imagination; Burke on the sublime and beautiful; Hogarth's analysis of beauty;

Mason's English garden; Wheatley's ornamental gardening; and Gilpin's picturesque views. Secondly by selecting and explaining admired passages from classical authors, as the Beauties of Shakespear, of Johnson, and of Stern. And lastly by exhibiting and explaining the prints of beautiful objects, or casts of the best antique gems and medallions.

The authors above mentioned have divided the objects of Taste into the sublime, the beautiful, and the new; but a new sect of inquirers into this subject have lately added the Picturesque; which is supposed to differ from the beautiful by it's want of smoothness, and from the sublime from it's want of size; but this circumstance has not yet perhaps undergone sufficient examination.—See essay on Picturesque, by U. Price.

Others have endeavoured to make a distinction between beauty and grace; and have esteem'd them, as it were, rivals for the possession of the human heart. But Grace may be defined Beauty in action; for a sleeping beauty can not be called graceful, in whatever attitude she may recline; the muscles must be in action to produce a graceful attitude, and the limbs to produce a graceful motion. The supposed origin of our ideas of beauty acquired in our early infancy from the curved lines, which form the female bosom,

bosom, is deliver'd in Zoonomia, vol. I. sect. xvi. 6; but is too metaphysical an investigation for young ladies.

Section XII.

DRAWING AND EMBROIDERY.

DRAWING as an elegant art belongs to the education of young ladies, and greatly facilitates the acquirement of Taste. As this is generally taught by masters, who profess it, I shall only observe, that tho' as an art it consists of deceiving the eye, yet as a science it is capable of producing to the mind the most sublime and beautiful images, or the most interesting scenes of life, for our amusement, admiration, or instruction.

The same observation applies to Embroidery, which is painting with the needle instead of the pencil, and seems to have been a fashionable employment of ladies of the highest rank in the early ages of the world. As the ladies in polite life have frequently much leisure time at their disposal, it is wise for them to learn many elegant as well as useful arts in their early years; which they may afterward cultivate for their amufement; and thus deprive folitude of irkfomenefs: And by being able to entertain themfelves, they may be lefs folicitous to enter the circles of diffipation, and depend lefs for happinefs on the caprice of others.

Befides the amufement or accomplifhment of poffeffing the talent of drawing, there is another advantage refulting from it; which confifts in ufing the pencil as a language to exprefs the forms of all vifible objects, as of flowers, machines, houfes, landfcapes; which can not in words alone be conveyed to others with fufficient accuracy: For this end it may be fufficient to draw in outlines alone the figures of natural things, without expending fo much time on this art, as is requifite to enable the learner to add the nice touches, which form the delicate gradations of fhade and colour.

It may be fuppofed, that fome knowledge of the fcience of perfpective fhould be previoufly acquired for the purpofe of drawing the outlines of objects; but I fufpect, that this is not always neceffary, fince at our learning to fee; before we have compared the ideas received by the fenfe of fight with thofe received by that of touch; any object placed before our eyes, as fuppofe the face of a companion, muft appear a flat coloured or fhaded furface,

face, and not a solid substance cover'd with eminences and depressions; as is so well proved by Bishop Berkley in his theory of vision. Hence if any one could so far unlearn the language of sight as to imagine the face of his companion to be a flat colour'd surface only, (as it is really seen) he would draw from nature as easily and exactly, as if he was copying a picture, as the inequalities would appear lights and shades; and he would thus be enabled to take the likeness with much greater facility and accuracy without the aid of the rules of perspective.

Section XIII.

THE HEATHEN MYTHOLOGY

Is connected with the study of taste, and should therefore be taught in boarding schools; as without some knowledge of it the works of the painters, statuarists, and poets, both antient and modern, can not be understood. But as a great part of this mythology consists of personify'd vices, much care should be taken in female schools, as well as in male ones, to prevent any bad impressions, which might be made on the mind by this kind

of

of erudition; this is to be accomplished by explaining the allegorical meaning of many of these supposed actions of heathen deities, and by shewing that they are at present used only as emblems of certain powers, as Minerva of wisdom, and Bellona of war, and thus constitute the language of painters; and are indeed almost the whole language which that art possesses, besides the delineation of visible objects in rest or in action.

These emblems however are not to be so easily acquired by descriptions alone, nor so easily remembered by young pupils; as when prints of antique statues, or medallions, or when cameos, or impressions of antique gems, are at the same time shewn and explained to them. For this purpose the prints of Spence's Polymetis may be exhibited and explained; from which Bell's pantheon is principally taken: And Dannet's dictionary of mythology, originally written in french, may be occasionally consulted; and the notes on Mr. Pope's translations of Homer.

There is also a little book intitled, "Instructions sur les Metamorphoses, par M. Le Ragois," which, I am informed is an useful and unexceptionable work for this purpose, containing a kind of summary of each story of fabulous mythology: to which may be added a translation of Ovid's Metamorphoses, published by Garth;

Garth; which, I am told, is the best translation of that work. Much agreeable knowledge of this kind is to be found in Byrant's mythology; Abbe de Pluche's history of the heavens; Warburton's essay on Elensinian mysteries; to which I beg leave to add the description of the Portland vase in the notes to the first volume of the Botanic garden.

Section XIV.

POLITE LITERATURE

MAY be divided into dissertations, plays, romances, poems; each of which, if the works are properly selected, may afford amusement and instruction to young persons; of some of the books of each of these classes of literature a catalogue will be given at the end of the work.

Such dissertations, as have been generally admired, may be selected from the Spectator, Tatler, Guardian, the World, the Rambler, Adventurer, besides many others.

Plays

Plays are of three kinds, tragical, sentimental, and humourous; of the first, Addison's Cato has been long admired; and the tragedies of Thompson consist of fine language. Of the second kind Cumberland's comedies are instances; and of the third Sheridan's comedies; some of which are entertaining and inoffensive, and may be read by young ladies without injury to their morals, or much outrage to their feelings.

There are many plays, which are better seen as exhibited on the stage, than as read in the closet; because the objectionable passages are generally omitted in the representation. But whether young ladies should be taught to act plays themselves, as is done at some boy's schools, is a matter of doubt. The danger consists in this, least the acquisition of bolder action, and a more elevated voice, should annihilate that retiring modesty, and blushing embarrasment, to which young ladies owe one of their most powerful external charms.

If young ladies act plays amongst themselves only, or without admitting more than two or three of their friends or parents; or if they repeat chosen scenes of plays, or speeches only, much of the above objection ceases, and some advantages may result to their attitudes or enunciation. Madam de Genlis's Theatre D'Educa-

D'Education affords the least exceptionable whole plays, with the sacred dramas of Miss Moore, and of Metastatio.

3. Novels or romances may be divided into the serious, the humorous, and the amorous. Of these, the use of the last should be intirely interdicted; but the first, when well managed, may convey instruction in the most agreeable and forceable manner: Such as Mr. Day's Sandford and Merton. The Children's friend. Tales of the castle. Robinson Crusoe. Edward, by the author of Zelucco. And to these may be added some other modern novels, the productions of ingenious ladies, which are I believe less objectionable than many others; as the Evelina, Cecilia, and Camilla of Miss Burney. The Emmeline and Ethelinda of Charlotte Smith; Inchbald's simple story; Mrs. Brook's Emely Montague; and the female Quixote; all which I have here introduced from the character given to me of them by a very ingenious lady, not having myself read them with sufficient attention. And lastly, the humorous novels, which are not written to inflame the passions, convey instruction, as far as they are imitations of real life: Of these are Le Sage's famous novel of Gil Blas; and Fielding's Tom Jones; neither of which however are proper books for young readers.

There are many, who condemn the use of novels altogether; but what are epic poems but novels in verse?—It is difficult to draw the line of limit between novels, and other works of imagination; unless the word novel be confined to mean only the romances of love and chivalry.

It is true indeed, that almost all novels, as well as plays, and epic poems, have some exceptional passages to be found in them; which might therefore be expunged, before they are allow'd to be read by young ladies. But are young women therefore to be kept in intire ignorance of mankind, with whom they must shortly associate, and from whom they are frequently to chuse a partner for life? This would be making them the slaves rather than the companions of men, like the Sultanas of a Turkish Seraglio. And how can young women, who are secluded from the other sex from their infancy, form any judgment of men, if they are not to be assisted by such books, as delineate manners? —A lady of fortune, who was persuaded by her guardian to marry a disagreeable and selfish man, speaking to her friend of the ill humour of her husband, lamented, that she had been prohibited from reading novels. " If I had read such books, said she, before " I was married, I should have chosen better; I was told, that " all men were alike except in respect to fortune."

We

We must however observe, that novels are perhaps more objectionable in schools than in private education; as the comments of one bad mind may be dangerous to the whole community: And as they are more amusing to young people than any other books, if read too early, they may give a distate to more useful knowledge; which are good reasons for the total prohibition of them in schools: And in private education, least a preference of fiction to truth should be thus instill'd, the ridiculous passages, with which even the best novels abound, should be carefully pointed out by a friend or governess; with their exaggerations, improbabilities, and frequent deviations from nature.

There are indeed few books, which delineate manners, whether in prose or poetry, however well chosen, which have not some objectionable passages in them. In reading the fables of Esop, Mr. Rousseau well observes, that the effect on the mind may frequently be totally different from that designed by the author; as in the fable where the fox flatters the crow, and gains the piece of cheese, the moral was designed to shew the folly of attending to flatterers; but may equally be supposed to applaud the cunning of the fox or flatterer, who is rewarded. In the popular narrative of Robinson Crusoe a childish superstition concerning intimations of future events, somewhat like the second fight of the highlands of Scotland, is frequently inculcated; and the use of rum or brandy is proposed as an infallible cure in all maladies; which however I am told is corrected in the new Robinson Crusoe.

Pamela, and Joseph Andrews, and Clarissa Harlow, are recommended by Madame de Genlis, and by Mrs. Macawley.—Madame de Genlis in a note in one of her works gives her reason for recommending Richardson's novels; because his heroins retain a more considerable degree of command over their affections than those of apparently less exceptionable romances. In this respect a novel call'd " Plain Sense," lately published by Lane, and written by an ingenious Cheshire lady, claims the preference to all others, and appears to me to carry this idea to excess.

The works of Richardson are nevertheless not only too voluminous, and thence would consume too much time, which might be better employ'd in schools; but in these, and even in Mr. Pope's rape of the lock, and his Eloisa to Abelard, many objectionable passages of another kind may be discover'd. If these passages, from which so few books are totally exempt, were expunged, it might raise curiosity, and induce young people to examine different copies of the same work, and to seek for other

impro-

improper books themselves; it is therefore perhaps better, when these books are read to a governess, that she should express disapprobation in a plain and quiet way of such passages, rather than to expunge them; which would give a feeling of dislike to the pupil, and confirm her delicacy, rather than give impurity to her ideas.

Much therefore depends on the conduct of the governess in this respect, so long as they are under the eye of a judicious monitor, no real harm could probably arise from their seeing human nature in all the classes of life, not only as it should be, or as it may be imagined to be, but as it really exists, since without comparison there can be no judgment, and consequently no real knowledge.

It must nevertheless be observed, that the excessive study of novels is universally an ill employment at any time of life; not only because such readers are liable to acquire a romantic taste; and to return from the flowery scenes of fiction to the common duties of life with a degree of regret; but because the high-wrought scenes of elegant distress display'd in novels have been found to blunt the feelings of such readers towards real objects of misery; which awaken only disgust in their minds instead of sentiments of pity or benevolence.

4. The

4. The works of the poets, as well as those of the writers of novels, require to be selected with great caution. The same may be said of painting, sculpture, and musick; which by delighting the imagination influence the judgment, and may thence be employ'd either to good or bad purposes: But as poetry, when thus selected, like painting, sculpture, and musick, it's rival sisters, is an object of refined taste, and affords an elegant amusement at least, it so far belongs to the education of young ladies.

Gay's fables, Thomson's seasons, Gisborne's walk in a forest, are proper for the younger classes of pupils; afterwards Pope's Ethic epistles, and essay on man, Goldsmith's poems, Akinside, Mason, Gray, and others, which are enumerated in the catalogue. I forbear to mention the Botanic garden; as some ladies have intimated to me, that the Loves of the plants are described in too glowing colours; but as the descriptions are in general of female forms in graceful attitudes, the objection is less forceable in respect to female readers. And besides the celebrated poets of our own country, as Milton and Shakespear, translations from the antients, as from Homer and Virgil; and from the more modern poems of Tasso, and Camoens, may be read with pleasure and improvement, tho' some objectionable passages may perhaps be found in all of them.

5. For

5. For the purpose of forming a style in writing, a few well-chosen books should be read often over; till the ear acquires, as it were, the musick of the sentences; and the imagination is thus enabled to copy it in our own compositions; such as those papers of the Spectator, which are ascribed to Addison, and are terminated with a capital letter of the word Clio; or some of Lady Wortley Montague's letters from Turkey; or other works of chaste, distinct, and expressive style, not over-loaded with metaphors, which with superabundance of ornament injure perspicuity.

But for other purposes of education it is perhaps better to teach young people select parts of many books, than a few intire ones; not only because the pupils will thus be acquainted with more authors in fashionable literature; but because the business of polite education is to give the outline of many species of erudition, or branches of knowledge; which the young ladies may cultivate further at their future leisure without the assistance of a teacher, as may best suit their tastes or their situations.

I cannot conclude this section on polite learning without mentioning, that some illiterate men have condemned the cultivation of the minds of the female sex, and have call'd such in ridicule

learned

learned ladies; as if it was a reproach to render themselves agreeable and useful. Where affectation is join'd with learning, it becomes pedantry, but this belongs oftener to the ignorant than to the cultivated; as is so well elucidated in "Letters to literary ladies," a small duodecimo published by Johnson, and written by one of the ingenious family of E—— in Ireland.

Section XV.

ARTS AND SCIENCES.

BESIDES the acquisition of grammar, languages, and common arithmetic; and besides a knowledge of geography, civil history, and natural history, there are other sciences, an outline of which might be taught to young ladies of the higher classes of the school, or of more inquiring minds, before or after they leave school; which might not only afford them present amusement, but might enable them at any future time to prosecute any of them further, if inclination and opportunity should coincide; and, by enlarging their sphere of taste and knowledge, would occasion them to be interested in the conversation of a greater number and of more ingenious men, and to interest them by their own conversation in return.

1. An outline of Botany may be learnt from Lee's introduction to botany, and from the translations of the works of Linnæus by a society at Lichfield; to which might be added Curtis's botanical magazine, which is a beautiful work, and of no great expence. But there is a new treatise introductory to botany call'd Botanic dialogues for the use of schools, well adapted to this purpose, written by M. E. Jacson, a lady well skill'd in botany, and published by Johnson, London. And lastly I shall not forbear to mention, that the philosophical part of botany may be agreeably learnt from the notes to the second volume of the Botanic garden, whether the poetry be read or not.

2. An outline of Chemistry, which surprizes and enchants us, may be learnt from the Elements of chemistry by Lavoisier, originally published in french; to which may be added a small work of Fourcroy call'd the philosophy of Chemistry. The former of these illustrious chemists perish'd by the guillotine, an irreparable loss to science and to mankind!

The acquirement of Chemistry should be preceded by a sketch

of Mineralogy; which is not only an interesting branch of science, as it teaches the knowledge of diamonds and precious stones, and of the various mines of metals, coals, and salt; but because it explains also the difference of soils, and is thus concern'd in the theory and practice of agriculture: But there is at present no proper introductory book, that I know of, on this subject for the use of children; as Cronstedt's, and Bergman's, and Kirwan's mineralogy are too exact and prolix; nor could be well understood without a small collection of fossils.

3. An outline of the sciences, to which Mathematics have generally been applied, as of astronomy, mechanics, hydrostatics, and optics, with the curious addition of electricity and magnetism, may best be acquired by attending the lectures in experimental philosophy, which are occasionally exhibited by itinerant philosophers; and which have almost exclusively acquired the name of natural philosophy.

The books in common use for teaching these sciences are too difficult and abstruse for the study of young persons. Some parts of natural phylosophy are render'd not unentertaining in the notes of the first volume of the Botanic garden, as the theory of meteors, and of winds; and an account of the strata of the earth; which

which neverthelefs require too much attention for very young ladies; but may be read with pleafure after leaving fchool by thofe, who poffefs inquiring minds. It is to be wifhed that fome writer of juvenile books would endeavour eafily to explain the ftructure and ufe of the barometer, and thermometer, and of clocks and watches, which fupply a part of the furniture of our houfes, and of our pockets.

4. In the fame manner the various arts and manufactories, which adorn and enrich this country, fhould occafionally be fhewn and explain'd to young perfons, as fo many ingenious parts of experimental philofophy; as well as from their immediately contributing to the convenience of life, and to the wealth of the nations, which have invented or eftablifhed them. Of thefe are the cotton works on the river Derwent in Derbyfhire; the potteries in Staffordfhire; the iron-founderies of Coalbrooke Dale in Shropfhire; the manufactories of Birmingham, Manchefter, Nottingham; but thefe are not in the province of a boarding fchool, but might be advantageoufly exhibited to young ladies by their parents in the fummer vacations.

5. In this fection of arts and fciences it may be proper to mention the art of producing a technical memory invented by

Mr. Gray; which may be readily acquired by consulting his book, and may perhaps be of advantage in remembering dates or numbers; as they are express'd by letters, and form'd into words. This work I attended to in my youth, but found it an amusing trick, rather than an useful art.

6. The art of writing Short-hand, which is said to be of English invention, should also be mentioned in this place. The book I learn'd this art from was publish'd by Gurney, and said to be an improvement on Mason; other treatises of short-hand I have also examined, but found them all nearly of equal excellence. I can only add, that many volumes, which I wrote from medical lectures, I now find difficult to decypher; and that as the words in short-hand are spelt from their sound only; those scholars, who practise this art early in life, are liable not afterwards to spell our language correctly; and lastly, that I believe, this art is still capable of improvement by first forming a more accurate alphabet, than that in common use among all european nations.

7. This section on arts and sciences may perhaps be thought to include more branches of them, than is necessary for female erudition. But as in male education the tedious acquirement of

antient

antient languages for the purpose of studying poetry and oratory is gradually giving way to the more useful cultivation of modern sciences, it may be of advantage to ladies of the rising generation to acquire an outline of similar knowledge; as they are in future life to become companions; and one of the greatest pleasures received in conversation consists in being reciprocally well understood. Botany is already a fashionable study for ladies; and chemistry is ingeniously recommended to them in the Letters to literary ladies.—Johnson, London.

Section XVI.

MORALS.

THE criterion of moral duties has been variously delivered by different writers: Expediency, by which is meant whatever increases the sum of public happiness, is by some called the criterion of virtue; and whatever diminishes that sum is term'd vice. By others the happiness or misery of the individual, if rightly understood, is said to be the bond of moral obligation. And lastly, by others the will of God is said to constitute the sole criterion of virtue and vice. But

But besides systematic books of morality, which are generally too abstruse for young minds, morals may be divided into five departments for the greater conveniency of the manner of instruction.

1. A sympathy with the pains and pleasures of others, or compassion.
2. A strict regard to veracity.
3. Prudence, justice, chastity.
4. Fortitude.
5. Temperance.

Section XVII.

COMPASSION.

A Sympathy with the pains and pleasures of others is the foundation of all our social virtues. "Do as you would be done by," is a precept, which descended from heaven. Whoever feels pain himself, when he sees others affected with it, will not only never be liable to give pain, but will always be inclined to relieve it. The lady, who possesses this christian virtue of compassion, cannot but be a good daughter, a good wife, and a good mother, that is, an amiable character in every department of life.

The manner of communicating this benevolent sympathy to children consists in expressing our own sympathy, when any thing cruel presents itself; as in the destruction of an insect; or when actions of cruelty are related in books or in conversation. I once observed a lady with apparent expressions of sympathy say to her little daughter, who was pulling off the legs of a fly, " how " should you like to have your arms and legs pull'd off? would it " not give you great pain? pray let it fly away out of the win- " dow:" which I doubt not would make an indelible impression on the child, and lay the foundation of an amiable character.

This virtue of compassion is a certain foundation of benevolence; and on that account renders children good to their own parents in the latter part of their lives, as well as to all other people; an important circumstance to the happiness of our latter years! Where cruelty or malevolence resides in the breast, it is generally exercised most by the child upon the aged parent, with whom in civilized society he frequently resides; and who often

lives

SECT. 17.   COMPASSION.

lives so long as to stand in his way to the possession of a wish'd-for inheritance.

This compassion, or sympathy with the pains of others, ought also to extend to the brute creation, as far as our necessities will admit; for we cannot exist long without the destruction of other animal or vegetable beings either in their mature or embryon state. Such is the condition of mortality, that the first law of nature is "eat, or be eaten." Hence for the preservation of our existence we may be supposed to have a natural right to kill those brute creatures, which we want to eat, or which want to eat us; but to destroy even insects wantonly shews an unreflecting mind, or a depraved heart.

A young gentleman once assured me, that he had lately fallen in love with a young lady; but, on their walking out one evening in summer, she took two or three steps out of her way on the gravel walk to tread upon an insect; and that afterwards whenever the idea of her came into his mind, it was attended with this picture of active cruelty; till that of the lady ceased to be agreeable, and he relinquished his design of courtship.

Nevertheless this sympathy, however amiable and necessary,

may

may be carried to an extreme, so as to render miserable the person, who possesses it; since many pitiable objects must be seen in our journey through life, which we have not power to relieve. This then furnishes us with a barrier or line, where to stop; that is, we should endeavour to render our little pupils alive to sympathize with all remediable evils; and at the same time to arm them with fortitude to bear the sight of such irremediable evils, as the accidents of life must frequently present before their eyes.

There should also be a plan in schools to promote the habit as well as the principle of benevolence; each young lady might occasionally contribute a small sum on seeing a needy naked child to purchase flannel or coarse linen for clothes, which they might learn to cut out, and to make up themselves; and thus the practise of industry might be united with that of liberality.

Another still more practical mode of producing a habit of benevolence in children might be by inducing them to employ some leisure hours in little works of taste, as in making artificial flowers, purses, fringes, and bestowing these on poor people, in order that they might sell them for their support. Miss Hartley at Bath, the daughter of the great medical philosopher of that name, has lately exhibited an amiable example of this kind of philanthropy; she has been long distinguished by her talents as an artist in painting; and has lately distributed her elegant performances among the poor famished emigrants, who reside in her neighbourhood; who are thus greatly assisted by the sale of her works.

Another channel, in which this sympathy should be taught to flow, is in the observance of those attentions, which perpetually diffuse happiness by promoting by courtesy of behaviour the cheerfulness, or forwarding by ready assistance the interests of those, whether equals, inferiors, or superiors; with whom every one happens to associate or reside: which constitutes the essential part of what is termed politeness of manners; and universally indicates a benevolent disposition.

Section XVIII.

VERACITY.

FOR the purpose of inculcating a love of truth early in life the love of praise supplies the most certain means. This kind of

SECT. 18.   VERACITY.   [51

honour has an honest pride for it's basis: a story is related in one of the modern volumes of the universal history of an inhabitant of Constantinople, who was brought to the scaffold for denying the divine mission of Mahomet; and on having a pardon offered him, if he would then declare his error, answer'd, that he would not speak an untruth to save his life. And, I think, it is recorded, that one of the fathers of the church used to affirm, that he would not tell a lie, were he sure to gain heaven by it.

I once heard an ingenious lady say to a company of her friends, that her daughter, a young girl, who stood by with a countenance flush'd with pleasure, never told her a lie in her life: This happy use of flattery was likely to produce a love for veracity, which would never be destroy'd by intersted motives.

The disgrace of telling a lie should be painted in vivid colours, as totally destructive of the character of a lady or gentleman, rendering them contemptible in the eyes of the world: And the inconvenience of this detestable habit of lying should be explain'd from it's preventing their being believed, when they wish it; as is exemplified in the fable of the shepherd-boy; who call'd out "the wolf, the wolf," so often to alarm his neighbours, and thus to amuse himself, when no wolf was near; that when the real wolf attack'd his flock, he could by no vociferation prevail on any one to come to his assistance: Or like the village-drunkard, who frequently amused himself with crying out " fire," along the streets on his return from the ale-house in the night, to the great alarm of the neighbourhood; till at length, when his cottage was really in flames, his distress was not believed, and he could gain no assistance to extinguish them.

This sincerity of character should be confirm'd by the example of the governesses, who should themselves pay the most exact and scrupulous attention to truth; they should not exaggerate trifling errors into reprehensible faults; and, where reproof is necessary, should give it with kindness: and should not only punctually fulfil their own promises, tho' to their inconvenience, but exact the same from their pupils in return.

To these should be added the precepts of religion, as soon as their minds are capable of receiving them, which uniformly inculcate truth and probity in all our words and actions.

Section XIX.

PRUDENCE, JUSTICE, CHASTITY.

THE impressions on the mind made by recent examples placed, as it were, before our eyes have so much more durable effects, than the more abstracted ideas deliver'd in systems of moral philosophy; that I believe the most efficacious method of inculcating the virtue of prudence in respect to their own conduct is by telling young people the ill consequences, which have lately happen'd to others; whose persons or names they are acquainted with: so that a repetition of the slander of a town, which always degrades the retailers, has sometimes it's advantage as a lesson to the hearers.

There is another kind of prudence, which it is necessary to acquire in some degree, which arms the possessor against the ill designs of others; hence they should be taught to beware of flatterers, gamesters, drunkards, and of all ill-temper'd persons. As this prudence is to be acquired by the knowledge of mankind, such books as the maxims of Rochfoucault, and others, might be recommended; but they give too gloomy a picture of human nature to be put into the hands of young ladies.

"Know yourself" is a celebrated injunction, and may constitute one department of Prudence, when any one undertakes some great action, or great change in the condition of life; but "know other people" is equally necessary in passing along this sublunary world, and may be inserted with propriety as another maxim in the code of prudence. The facility of knowing others in the daily intercourse of the world is produced by the knowledge of physiognomy, acquired at schools in early life; while the passions continue to be impress'd on the countenances of children; and which is never so well acquired in private tuition; and thus constitutes one of the great advantages of school-education.

JUSTICE and CHASTITY, which are the principal links, by which civilized society is held together, are to be inculcated in young minds by similar methods; that is by pointing out by examples the public punishment, or public disgrace, which certainly accompanies the breach of either of these important duties: and afterwards to add the precepts of religon, when their minds are capable

capable of perceiving their force, to co-operate with the effect of the laws of society, and of the opinion of the wise and virtuous.

Section XX.

FORTITUDE.

IF female children are not treated with tenderness by a mother in their early years of infancy, they are perhaps liable to acquire a harshness of character, and an apparent unfeelingness, which afterwards renders them less amiable; though it may give them greater fortitude; which should therefore be inculcated at their rather maturer years.

Neither the robust assailing courage, which prompts to the performance of heroic actions, nor the ostentatious patience, which requires the flattery of the public eye for its's support, belong to the female character. But that serene strength of mind, which faces unavoidable danger with open eyes, prepared to counteract or to bear the necessary evils of life, is equally valuable

able as a male or female acquisition. This is term'd presence of mind; it depends on our judgment of the real value of things; and on our application of those causes, which contribute to turn disagreeable circumstances to the best advantage; and can therefore only be acquired by the general cultivation of good sense and of knowledge.

An occasional effusion of tears has been thought an amiable weakness, and a mark of delicacy of the sex. When tears are shed at the irremediable misfortunes of others, it indicates an amiable sensibility; but when young ladies indulge themselves in a promptitude of dissolving into incessant tears at every trivial distress of their own, it shews a kind of infantine debility of mind, and conveys an idea of their being unfit for the common duties of life; and should therefore be discouraged by reasoning on the kind and quantity of the evil, which disturbs them; and by reciting to them the examples of fortitude exhibited by others in disasters much more calamitous, of which there are examples in the letters of Lady Russel: And lastly by reminding them of the consolations of religion.

A slight appearance of timidity has been esteem'd another mark of delicacy of the sex; but timidity is the companion of debility

debility of mind rather than of delicacy, and should not therefore be encouraged. In respect to the expressions of fear the violent cries and distorted countenances of some ladies in situations of danger exhibit them in no very amiable attitudes; while they increase the confusion, and may be said "to help the storm;" but if to these be added an affectation of fear without cause; as when a young lady screams through the whole gamut at the sight of a spider, or a grass-hopper; the fault becomes voluntary, and should be opposed and conquer'd by the shafts of ridicule.

Impudence in common language has been termed boldness; and bashfulness has been ascribed to timidity; but neither of them with sufficient precision; as brave men have been known to be bashful, and cowards impudent. Assurance of countenance arises from the possessor of it rather over-valuing his own abilities; and impudence consists in this assurance with a total disregard of the opinions of others; but neither of them bear any analogy to fortitude. On the other hand modesty arises from the possessor of it rather under-valuing his own abilities; and bashfulness consists in this modesty with great solicitude about the opinions of others; but neither of them are attended with personal fear. So charming is the appearance of this great sensibility by adding a blush to the features of beauty, that no endeavours should be used to extinguish it early in life. Nor should any means be contrived to increase it to excess, as embarrassment both of thought and action, and even impediment of speech, is then liable to attend the great anxiety it occasions.

Section XXI.

TEMPERANCE

INCLUDES the subjugation of the appetites and passions to reason and prudence; it consists in our moderation in the use of all those things, which contribute to the convenience, comfort, or enjoyment of life; as of food, dress, pleasures; and in the restraining our licentious passions, as of anger, vanity, love, ambition. The method to instil this virtue is by exhibiting the various inconveniences, which attend unlimitted indulgence; and thus to inculcate the golden rule of "nothing to excess."

The example of the governess will have great effect in producing many of the virtues above mention'd in the minds of her pupils. Justice in the most trivial circumstance must be carefully

and

and exactly done between children in respect to each other in their little disputes at play. Moderation and self-government should also constantly appear in the characters of those, who are to teach these virtues to others.

Section XXII.

RELIGION.

THE precepts of religion are best taught by requiring the young pupils regularly to attend such places of divine worship, as their parents direct; and by reading on sundays select parts of the holy scriptures, and some approved books of sermons; as those of Blair, and a few others; and by inculcating the reasonableness of daily thanksgiving, and the duty of daily prayer, to the great author of all good.

The divine morality deliver'd in the new testament should be repeatedly inculcated to an infant audience, who cannot so well understand the metaphysical parts of religion, such as the duty of doing to others as we would they should do unto us: to love our neighbours as ourselves: to forgive injuries, not to revenge them: and to be kind even to our enemies. For this purpose the sermons of the old Whole duty of man are recommended; one of which might be read every sunday evening.

Ladies of more mature years, or who have finished their school-education, may learn the necessity and usefulness of our excellent religion from Baron Haller's letters to his daughter, from Lady Pennington's advice to her daughter, and lastly from Mr. Gisborne's duties of the female sex: and the defence of the truth of it may be learn'd from Mr. Paley's evidences of christianity; but perhaps it is better for them not to perplex their minds with many works of religious controversy.

Section XXIII.

ADDRESS.

THERE is a fascinating manner in the address of some people, which almost instantly conciliates the good will, and even the confidence of their acquaintance. Machiavel in his history of Castruccio Castricani observes; that his hero could assume such openess of countenance; that though he was known to be a man practised in every kind of fraud and treachery, yet in a few minutes he gain'd the confidence of all, whom he conversed with; they went away satisfied of his good will towards them, and were betrayed to their ruin.

This enviable address, which may be used for good purposes as well as for bad ones, may be difficult to analize; but may possibly consist simply in a countenance animated with pleasure at meeting and conversing with our acquaintance; and which diffuses cheerfulness by pleasurable contagion into the bosoms of others; and thus interests them in our behalf. It is not the smile of flattery, nor the smile of self-approbation, nor the smile of habit, nor of levity; but it is simply an expression of pleasure, which seems to arise at the sight of our acquaintance; and which persuades them, that they possess our love, and for which they barter their own in return.

However this conciliating manner may have been used, as above related, for bad purposes; it probably proceeded originally from friendliness and openess of heart, with cheerful benevolence; and that in those, who have in process of time become

bad

bad characters, the appearance of those virtues has remain'd, after the reality of them has vanish'd. What then is the method, by which this inchantment of countenance can be taught? certainly by instilling cheerfulness and benevolence into the minds of young ladies early in life, and at the same time an animation of countenance in expressing them; and though this pleasurable animation be at first only copied, it will in time have the appearance of being natural; and will contribute to produce by association the very cheerfulness and benevolence, which it at first only imitated. This is a golden observation to those, who have the care of young children.

A very accomplish'd lady, who read the manuscript of this work, wrote the following with her pencil on the opposite page: " nothing can be more just and interesting than the whole of this section; yet however desirable it may be to mend an unpleasant *abord,* might one not suspect, since Nature has produced a diversity of manner, that an attempt to engraft this beautiful cheerfulness on a grave set of features might produce the worst of evil affectations? A natural simplicity of manner, whether serious or gay, will always please; and probably this amiable address may be rendered equally consistent with natural manners, whether serious or gay."

Section

Section XXIV.

CONVERSATION.

NEXT to the winning manners above described, the art of pleasing in conversation seems to consist in two things; one of them to hear well; and the other to speak well. The perpetual appearance of attention, and the varying expression of the countenance of the hearer to the sentiments or passions of the speaker, is a principal charm in conversation; to be well heard and accurately understood encourages our companions to proceed with pleasure, whatever may be the topics of their discourse.

Those, who have been educated at schools, and have learnt the knowledge of physiognomy from their playfellows in their early years, understand the pleasurable or painful feelings of all with whom they converse, often even before their words are finished; and, by thus immediately conforming the expression of their own features to the sensations of the speaker, become the interesting and animated companions above described, which is

seldom

seldom seen in those educated in private families; and which, as before observed, gives a preference to school-education.

To speak agreeably in respect to manner consists in a voice clear, yet not loud; soft, yet not plaintive; with distinct articulation, and with graceful attitudes rather than with graceful actions; as almost every kind of gesticulation is disagreeable. In respect to the matter it should be such, as coincides with the tastes or pursuits of those, to whom the conversation is address'd. From hence it will appear, that both to hear well, and to speak well, requires an extensive knowledge of things, as well as of the tastes and pursuits of mankind; and must therefore ultimately be the effect of a good education in general, rather than a particular article of it.

There are however faults to be avoided, and cautions to be observed, in the conversation of young ladies; which should be pointed out to them by the governess of a boarding school. Of these I shall mention first, that whenever the thirst of shining in conversation seizes on the heart, the vanity of the speaker becomes apparent; and we are disgusted with the manner, whatever may be the matter of the discourse.

Secondly,

Secondly, that it is always childish, and generally ridiculous, when young people boast of their follies, or when they accuse themselves of virtues; neither of which they probably possess in the degree, which they describe. A young lady was heard to say, " I am frighten'd to death at the sight of a bird:" And another, that she was so inconsiderate, as to give her money to the poor naked children, whom she saw in the streets in winter.

Thirdly, they should be apprized, that there is danger in speaking ill even of a bad person; both because they may have been misinform'd, and because they should judge their neighbours with charity. A friend of mine was once ask'd by a young man, how he could distinguish, whether the lady, whom he meant to address, was good temper'd; and gave this answer. " When any dubious accusation is brought in conversation against an absent person; if she always inclines to believe the worst side of the question, she is ill-temper'd." There are some nice distinctions on this subject of good nature delivered in Lady Pennington's advice to her daughters, p. 89, which are worth a young lady's attention.

Fourthly, that it is dangerous for a young lady to speak very highly in praise even of a deserving man; for if she extols his actions,

actions, she will seem to give herself the importance of a judge, and her determinations will sometimes be call'd in question; and to commend highly the person of a man is in general estimation inconsistent with the delicacy of the sex at any age.

Fifthly, young ladies should be advised not to accustom themselves to the use of strong asseverations, or of a kind of petty oaths, such as " upon my honour," in their conversation; nor often to appeal to others for the truth of what they affirm; since all such strong expressions and appeals derogate somewhat from the character of the speaker; as they give an intimation, that she has not been usually believed on her simple assertion.

Sixthly, laughing vehemently aloud, or tittering with short shrieks, in which some young ladies, who have left school, indulge themselves at cards or other amusements, are reprehensible; as their dignity of character must suffer by appearing **too violently** agitated at trivial circumstances.

Seventhly, an uniform adherence to sincerity in **conversation** is of the first importance; as without it our words are but empty sounds, and can no more interest our companions than the tinkling of a bell. No artificial polish of manners can compensate for the

apparent

apparent want of this virtue, nor any acquirements of knowledge for the reality of the want of it. Hence though the excefs of blame or praife of the actions of others may be imprudent or improper in the converfation of young ladies; as mentioned in the third and fourth articles of this fection; yet in thefe, as in all other kinds of converfation, their opinions fhould be given with truth, if given at all; but when the characters of others are concern'd, they fhould be delivered with diffidence and modefty.

Laftly, if at any time any improper difcourfe fhould be addrefs'd to young ladies, which has a tendency to indecency, immorality, or irreligion, they fhould be taught to exprefs a marked difapprobation both in words and countenance. So great is the power of the fofter fex in meliorating the characters of men; that, if fuch was their uniform behaviour, I doubt not, but that it would much contribute to reform the morals of the age; an event devoutly to be wifhed, and which would contribute much to their own happinefs.

To thefe might be added many other obfervations from the writers on female education, concerning a due refpect in converfation to fuperiors, good temper to equals, and condefcenfion to inferiors. But as young ladies are not expected to fpeak with the wisdom, or precision of philosophers; and as the careless cheerfulness of their conversation, with simplicity of manner, and with the grace, ease, and vivacity natural to youth, supplies it with it's principal charms; these should be particularly encouraged, as there are few artificial accomplishments, which could compensate for the loss of them.

Section XXV.

EXERCISE.

THE acquirements of literature, and of many arts, make the lives of young people too sedentary; which impairs their strength, makes their countenances pale and bloated, and lays the foundation of many diseases; hence some hours should every day be appropriated to bodily exercises, and to relaxation of mind.

Such as tend to produce activity, and to promote the growth of the person in respect to height, are prefer'd in the schools for young ladies to those, which render the system more robust and muscular.

Of these playing at ball, at shuttlecock, swinging as they sit on a cord or cushion, and dancing, in the open air in summer, and within doors in winter, are to be prefer'd. To these some have recommended an exercise of the arms by swinging leaden weights, which are call'd dumb bells; these should be very light, if they be used at all, otherwise they load the spine of the back, and render the shoulders thick and muscular, and rather impede than forward the perpendicular growth of the person. The ringing of a real bell hung as is done in churches, or the frequent drawing up of a weight by a cord over a pulley, with a fly-wheel to prevent it's too hasty descent, would be an exercise, which might be used with great advantage by young people; as it both extends the spine, and strengthens the muscles of the chest and arms.

Many other kinds of exercise have been recommended by authors: Madam Genlis advises weights to be carried on the head, as milk-maids carry their milk-pails; and even to add weights to the soles of the shoes of children to strengthen, as she supposes, the muscles of locomotion in walking or running. It is evident, that carrying weights on the head must be injurious to young people, especially where there is a tendency to softness of the bones; as it may contribute to bend the spine by their pressure

sure, and to impede the perpendicular growth of the body; and the walking in weighted shoes may induce awkward gestures without any adequate advantage.

There are other modes of exertion, which, though graceful in themselves, are not allow'd to ladies by the fashion of this age and country; as skating on the ice in winter, swimming in summer, funambulation, or dancing on the streight rope: but walking with a stately measured step occasionally, like the march of soldiers, and reading aloud frequently rather in a theatric manner, as well as dancing and singing, will much contribute to give strength and grace to the muscles of locomotion, and of vocallity.

Section XXVI.

AIR.

THE strength and activity of young people not only depends on the perpetual exercise of their limbs, as described in the preceding sections, but on the purity of the air, which they breathe, and

even

even on the occasional coldness of it. The cold air of winter acts on delicate people like a cold bath; as it diminishes the action of the subcutaneous vessels for a time, and thus produces an accumulation of animal power, whence an increased action of those vessels and a consequent warmth of the surface of the body succeeds; and by this less expenditure of animal power during immersion in cold air, and it's consequent accumulation, the person becomes stronger for a time and more animated; which is termed in common language " bracing the system." Hence to strengthen delicate children they should be encouraged to go into the cold air of winter frequently, but should not remain in it longer than a quarter or half an hour at a time. In summer young people can scarcely continue too much in the air, where they are shaded from the heat of the sun.

A constant immersion in pure air is now known to contribute much both to the health of the system, and to the beautiful colour of the complexion. And this atmosphere should undergo a perpetual change and renovation; that the vital air, which constitutes about one-fourth part of it, may not be too much diminished by frequent respiration. Due attention should be given to this important circumstance both by frequently urging the young ladies to amuse themselves out of doors; and by the proper venti-

lation

lation of the school-room, dining-room, bed-rooms, and their other apartments. For this purpose it is convenient to saw off about one inch from the top of every door of these crowded rooms, and opposite to this aperture to nail along the top of the door a tin plate about two inches wide, rising at an angle of about forty-five degrees; which will bend the current of air up towards the ceiling; where it will be mixed with the warm air of the room, and sink down amongst the society without the danger of giving cold to any one: And, besides these door-ventilators, the upper sashes of every window should always be let down a few inches, when the external weather will admit of it.

In respect to bed-rooms, which have more than one bed, the doors should be furnished with similar ventilators for the due admission of fresh air; and during the summer months a window should be kept a few inches open during the night as well as the day; the sash of which should have a bolt or other proper fastening for this purpose; nor should the fire-place be stopt up at any season by a chimney board, or a bag of straw; as many rooms are made to shut up so close, that this is the only aperture, by which fresh air is admitted. To this should be added, that the bed curtains should never be drawn close round the beds; which confine the air spoil'd by frequent respiration, and the perspirable matter,

like

like a noxious atmosphere over the unconscious sleepers. At the same time none of the beds should be placed very near either to an open window, or to an open chimney, as a partial current of air might be injurious by the coldness it might occasion.

In crowded bed-rooms, where children are close shut up for eight or nine hours every night, not only the pale bloated complexion, which is seen in children of crowded manufactories; but other diseases are produced by the impurity of the air, such as indigestion, difficulty of breathing, and sometimes convulsive fits, as mention'd in Zoonomia, vol. II. class iii. 1. 1. 5. and lastly putrid fevers; of which fatal instances frequently occur in the crowded habitations of the poor. Hence parents cannot be too careful in inspecting the bed-rooms, and the beds of the schools, to which they intrust their children; as not only their present comfort, but their future health, and sometimes their lives depend on this attention; as is further explain'd in the section on rheumatism.

Besides the due ventilation of rooms by a perpetual supply of pure air in summer, something should be here said about the manner of warming them in winter. As the quantity of air carried up a chimney is very great, owing to it's being render'd so much lighter than the external atmosphere by the heat of the fire, strong currents of cold air press into the room at every chink of the doors and windows passing towards the fire; and are liable to give catarrh, rheumatism, kibed heels, and swelled fingers to those scholars, who are exposed to them. To lessen these currents of cold air setting in at every aperture, the chimney should be so contracted over the fire-grate, as to admit no more of the warm air to go up it, than is necessary to carry up the smoke; and hence much more of the warm air near the fire-place will rise up to the ceiling; and descending, as it becomes cooler, in the distant parts of the room, will form a kind of vertical eddy, and warm the whole appartment; adding greatly to the heat produced by the radiation from the fire.

To effect this Doctor Franklin recommended an iron or tin plate to slide under the mantle-piece over the fire, so as to contract the aperture of the chimney to two or three inches in width, all the length over the fire-grate. And lately Count Rumford has accomplish'd the same purpose by a flat stone about twelve inches broad, and eighteen inches high; which is rear'd upon one end at the back of the fire-place, about eight inches above the grate, and leans forward towards the mantle-piece, so as to leave an aperture, three or four inches wide, and twelve or four-

teen

teen inches long, over the front of the fire-place. The use of both these contrivances is to contract the mouth of the chimney, and thus to admit no more warm air up it, than is necessary to convey the smoke. And the sliding iron plate in Franklin's plan, and the end-reared stone in Rumford's plan, are designed to be occasionally withdrawn for the admittance of the chimney-sweeper. These are described in detail in the essays of Doctor Franklin, and Count Rumford; and it is believed, that one-third of the fuel may be thus saved, and the rooms be kept more equally warm, and more salutary.

Section XXVII.

CARE OF THE SHAPE.

DELICATE young ladies are very liable to become awry at many boarding schools, this is occasion'd principally by their being obliged too long to preserve an erect attitude, by sitting on forms for many hours together. To prevent this the school-seats should either have backs, on which they may occasionally rest themselves; or desks before them, on which they may occasionally lean. This is a thing of greater confequence, than may appear to thofe, who have not attended to it; and who wifh their children to acquire a very erect attitude.

When the leaft tendency to become awry is obferved, they fhould be advifed to lie down on a bed or fofa for an hour in the middle of the day for many months; which generally prevents the increafe of this deformity by taking off for a time the preffure of the head and neck and fhoulders on the fpine of the back; and it at the fame time tends to make them grow taller.

Young perfons, when nicely meafured, are found to be half an inch higher in the morning than at night; as is well known to thofe, who inlift very young men for foldiers. This is owing to the cartilages between the bones of the back becoming comprefs'd by the weight of the head and fhoulders on them during the day. It is the fame preffure, which produces curvitures and diftortions of the fpine in growing children, where the bones are fofter than ufual; and which may thus be relieved by an horizontal pofture for an hour in the middle of the day, or by being frequently allow'd to lean on a chair, or to play on a carpet on the ground.

Young ladies should also be directed, where two sleep in a bed, to change every night, or every week, their sides of the bed; which will prevent their tendency to sleep always on the same side; which is not only liable to produce crookedness, but also to occasion diseases by the internal parts being so long kept in uniform contact as to grow together. For the same reason they should not be allow'd to sit always on the same side of the fire or window; because they will then be inclined too frequently to bend towards one side; which in those constitutions, where the bones are too soft, is liable to produce crookedness of the spine.

Another great cause of injury to the shape of young ladies is from the pressure of stays, or other tight bandages; which at the same time cause other diseases by changing the form or situation of the internal parts. If a hard part of the stays, even a knot of the thread, with which they are sewed together, is press'd upon one side more than the other; the child bends from the side, which is uneasy, and thus occasions a curiviture of the spine. To counteract this effect such stays, as have fewest hard parts, and especially such as can be daily or weekly turn'd, are preferable to others. A wise fashion of wearing no stiff stays, which

adds

adds so much to the beauty of young ladies, has commenced since the above was written; and long may it continue!

Where frequent lying down on a sofa in the day time, and swinging frequently for a small time by the head, with loose dress, do not relieve a beginning distortion of the back, I have used with some success a swing for children to sleep in, as described in Zoonomia, vol. II. class I. 2. 2. 16. and also a crutch-chair, as there delineated; and where these do not seem to succeed, recourse may also be had to Monsf. Vacher's spinal machine, first described in the memoirs of the academy of Surgery in Paris, vol. III. with a good print of it; and since made by Mr. Jones in London, at No. 6, North-street, Tottenham-court Road; which suspends the head, and places the weight of it on the hips.

It will be from hence easily perceived, that all other methods of confining or directing the growth of young people should be used with great skill, such as back-boards, or bandages; and that their application should not be continued too long at a time; least worse consequences should ensue, than the deformity they are designed to remove. Of these the stocks for the feet of children, for the purpose of making them turn their toes quite out, and

SECT. 27. CARE OF THE SHAPE. 79]

the frame for pressing in their knees, as they stand erect, at the same time, I suspect, when carried to excess, to be particularly injurious, and to have caused an irrecoverable lameness of the hip-joint; as explain'd in Zoonomia, vol. II. class I. 2. 2. 17. These therefore should be used with proper caution, so as to give no pain or uneasy feels, or not used at all.

To this it may be proper to add, that the stiff erect attitude, taught by some modern dancing masters, does not contribute to the grace of person, but rather militates against it; as is well seen in one of the prints in Hogarth's analysis of beauty; and is exemplify'd by the easy grace of some of the antient statues, as of the Venus de Medici, and the Antinous; and in the works of some modern artists, as in a beautiful print of Hebe feeding an eagle, painted by Hamilton, and engraved by Eginton; and many of the figures of Angelica Kauffman. And lastly, which is so eminently seen in many of the beauties of the present day, since they have left off the constraint of whale-bone stays, and assumed the graceful dress of the ancient grecian statues.

In the tendency to curviture of the spine whatever strengthens the general constitution is of service, as the use of the cold bath in the summer months. This however requires some restriction

both

both in respect to the degree of coldness of the bath, the time of continuing in it, and the season of the year. Common springs, which are of 48 degrees of heat, are too cold for tender constitutions, whether of children or adults; and frequently do them great and irreparable injury, as I have witnessed in three or four cases. The coldness of river water in the summer months, which is about 65 degrees, or that of Matlock, which is about 68, or of Buxton, which is 82, are much to be prefer'd: The two latter are improperly call'd warm baths, comparing their degree of heat with that of common springs; whereas they are in reality cold baths, being of much lower degree of heat than that of the human body, which is 98. The time of continuing in a cold bath should be but a few minutes; certainly not so long as to occasion a trembling of the limbs from cold. In respect to the season of the year, delicate children should certainly only use cold bathings in the summer months; as the going frequently into the cold air in winter will answer all the purposes of the cold bath.

Other means of counteracting the debility of the system, or softness of bones, which occasion crookedness, consist in taking internally from 10 to 20 grains of extract of bark, with as much soda phosphorata, and mix'd with from five to ten drops of tincture of opium, twice a day for three or four weeks; as is further treated of in Zoonomia, vol. II. class I. 2. 2. 14. and 16.

Section XXVIII.

DRESS.

YOUNG Ladies should be instructed to shew attention to their dress, as it gives an idea of cleanliness of their persons; which has so great a charm, that it may be reckon'd amongst the inferior virtues; for this purpose an elegant simplicity of dress is to be recommended in preference to that superabundance of ornament, where the lady herself is the least part of her. The form of dress must nevertheless perpetually vary with the fashion of the time; but a person of taste may lessen those parts of a fashionable dress, which oppose beauty or grace; and bring forwards those, which are more coincident with them; so as to wear a dress in fashion, and yet not devoid of taste.

Thus when large hoops were in general use, which so totally militate with all ideas of beauty and grace; ladies of taste wore them as small, as custom would allow. So in respect to the ear-rings of the present day; since piercing the tender part of the ear for the purpose of suspending a weight of gold, or of precious stones, or of glass beads to it, reminds us of the savage state of mankind; those ladies of taste, who think themselves obliged to comply with this indecorous fashion, use the lightest materials, as a chain of small pearls, to give a less distressing idea of the pain, they seem to suffer at every motion of their heads. Hence also long pendant and complicated ear-rings, however they may add to the dignity of riper years by their costliness, are unbecoming to young ladies; as they seem to give pain in the quicker, tho' more graceful, motions of juvenility.

Sir Joshua Reynolds, I think, observes in one of his addresses to the academy, that hard curls of hair stiffen'd with the fat of hogs, and cover'd with the flower of wheat, cannot be admitted into picture. The same may be observed of that coat of mail, the whale-bone stays, the use of which is now so happily discontinued. Both of these, however they may conceal the grey hairs and waining figures of those, who are advanced in life, are highly injurious to the flowing locks and graceful forms of young ladies.

As

SECT. 28. DRESS.

As beauty confifts of lines flowing in eafy curves according to the analyfis of Hogarth; thofe parts of drefs, which are compofed of fuch lines, are always agreeable. Thus a fafh defcending from one fhoulder to the oppofite hip, or a grecian veil thrown back and winding carelefsly down behind, are always beautiful; but a few white oftrich feathers rifing on the head before, and a train of filk fweeping on the ground behind, add fo much grace to a moving female figure, as to attract all eyes with unceafing admiration.

In moving forwards the hair falls back, and in very fwift motion floats upon the air behind; hence by affociation of ideas, when the hair is made to retire from the cheeks, it gives an intimation of the youthful agility of the perfon; and when it is brought forwards over the cheeks, it may confent with unmoving dignity, like the full wig of a judge, but diminifhes our idea of the activity of playful youth.

Where the appearance of ufe in drefs can be given to ornaments, it fuggefts an excufe for wearing them, and is therefore to be prefer'd; as diamond pins, ftrings of pearl, and a comb of fhell, to reftrain the exuberant hair; or knots of ribbons to fix the flipper on the foot, to contract the fleeve around the arm, to unite the veſt upon the boſom, or to attach the cap above the forehead. And when theſe are ſimilar in colour, it gives an air of ſimplicity, and a kind of pyramidal form to the dreſs; which the painters ſo much endeavour to exhibit both in their landſcapes, and their groups of figures.

Other ornaments, which bear no analogy to uſe in dreſs, ſhould be ſparingly worn; leaſt they give an idea, that they were deſign'd to diſplay the pride of the poſſeſſor, rather than to decorate her perſon. Theſe are ſometimes ſeen ſo ill placed as to make deformities conſpicuous, as a number of rings on fingers diſtorted with the gout, or ſplendid buckles on turn'd-in feet. Where there is no appearance of uſe, all ſhining ornaments ſhould be ſo diſpoſed as to direct the eye of the beholder to ſome beautiful feature of the lady, who wears them; as diamond ſtars in the hair, and artificial flowers on the boſom.

Paint and perfumes are totally inadmiſſible in the dreſs of young ladies, as they give a ſuſpicion of natural defects in reſpect to colour of the ſkin, and odour of the breath. Where there exiſts but a mediocrity of beauty, and youth is in the wain, a variety of pretty or of coſtly ornaments on the dreſs, and even the whiteneſs of powder in the hair, may ſometimes mingle with

our

our idea of the person, and seem to render the whole fairer, more pleasing, or more respectable. But ornaments of every kind are useless or injurious to youthful beauty; they add no power to the charm, but rather disenchant the beholder by abstracting his attention; which dwells with undiminish'd rapture on beauty array'd by simplicity, and animated without affectation. Thus the majestic Juno of Homer is array'd in variety of ornament, and with ear-rings, which have three large pendant bobs to each, and commands universal homage. But his Queen of Beauty is dress'd with more simple elegance, in her magic sash, or cestus, and charms all eyes.

The attention to taste in dress may nevertheless be carried into an extreme; it should not seem to be the most important part of the education of a young lady; or the principal object of her care; she should rather appear to follow than to lead the fashion, according to the lines of Mr. Pope,

> Be not the first, on which the new are tried,
> Nor yet the last to lay the old aside.

Section XXIX.

AMUSEMENTS

ARE generally diftinguifh'd from exercife, as they relieve or exhilerate the mind. Cards may be occafionally ufed by children in private families, without their gaming for money; and will in general facilitate their acquirement of arithmetic; but cannot be allow'd in fchools, leaft the young ladies fhould expend too much time upon them, or fhould play for money clandeftinely. But the game of chefs, from its bearing fo great analogy to common life, is fuppofed much to improve the moft ufeful powers of the mind: It has the experience of the remoteft antiquity to recommend it, occafions no depraved paffions, as it is not play'd for money; and by the caution perpetually neceffary to watch your adverfary, and the judgment required to contrive, arrange, and manage your own affairs, employs and ftrengthens every part of the underftanding.

Embroidery, drawing, music, as well as the exercises of dancing, swinging, playing at ball, and shuttlecock, should be class'd amongst the amusements of young ladies; and should be reciprocally applied to, either in the house or in the open air, for the purpose of relieving each other; and of producing by such means an uninterrupted cheerfulness of mind; which is the principal charm, that fits us for society, and the great source of earthly happiness.

Section XXX.

PUNISHMENTS. REWARDS. MOTIVES.

It is the custom of many schools to use some kinds of punishments, which either give pain or disgrace to the delinquent, as a fool's cap, or a meal of water gruel. The use of these are seldom if ever necessary in schools for young ladies, and are always attended with disagreeable consequences, as they either diminish the character of honour in the punish'd persons, sink their spirits, or render them insensible to the opinions of others; or injure their health: Insomuch that at some schools all that can be acquired can scarcely compensate the loss of cheerfulness, and degradation of mind, or bad health, which their punishments produce.

Thus the sitting in the public school for an hour in a cap with bells diminishes the sensibility of a child to the opinions of her companions, and thus gradually destroys one of the greatest motives to good actions, and of the greatest restraints from bad ones. For the same reason reprimands and even admonitions should be always applied in private, but applause or reward in public.

A meal of water gruel, given as a punishment instead of a meal of animal food, so frequently had recourse to in some boarding schools, I believe to have laid the foundation of incurable debility. The diseases of debility, as scrophula, bronchocele, softness of bones, and the consequent distortion of them, are very common among the children of the poor in Derby, which on examination, I believe to be owing to their food consisting chiefly of gruel; or sometimes with milk, which has been twice skim'd, so that it is totally deprived of it's most nourishing part; at other times with weak salt broth, but seldom with solid animal food. When broth is weak in respect to the quantity of fleshmeat boil'd in it, it is the custom of cooks to add much salt to it to increase the relish, which renders it still more injurious to weak children;

as salt contains no nourishment, and by its stimulus increases the action of the system; and by promoting great insensible or sensible perspiration diminishes the strength of the child more, than the small quantity of meat dissolved in the broth can counterbalance.

2. How then are refractory children to be govern'd? certainly by the superiority of the mind of the teacher over that of the pupil. When a famous lady in Italy was put to the torture, and question'd by what sorcery she had govern'd a princess of the family of Medici; she answer'd " by no sorcery, but by that power, which superior minds possess over inferior ones."

3. Besides the two circumstances, which so much govern the great world, I mean hope of reward and fear of punishment; in the microscosm of a boarding school blame and praise, if given very sparingly, will be found strong motives to the little pupils to perform their tasks well, and of more efficacy ten times, than the meal of water gruel, or the disgrace of a cap and bells. Esteem and disgrace are observed by Mr. Locke to be of all others the most powerful incentives to the mind, when once it is brought to regard them: And if once you can communicate to children a love of credit, and an apprehension of shame, you have

instill'd

instill'd into them a principle, which will constantly act, and incline them to do right, tho' it is not the true source from whence our actions ought to spring; which should be from our duty to others and to ourselves.—See Essay on education, sect. 56, &c. where are many other valuable observations on this subject.

4. Emulation at seeing others excel, if properly managed is another incitement to industry. But as this is liable to degenerate into envy, it should rather be left to it's own operation, than be promoted by pointing out the examples, which should be copied. It is better to say, " your task is not done to-day so well as you sometimes do it," than to say, " your task is not done so well as your sister's." Since in the latter case envy, and it's consequence hatred, may succeed; a thing of tenfold worse consequence than the neglect of a thousand tasks.

5. Tho' some degree of flattery may be used with success in teaching veracity to very young children, as mention'd in sect. 18. of this work, yet I think it should be used very rarely indeed, and only on very important occasions, least it should become a necessary motive of action, instead of moral duty; as observed in Zoonomia, vol. II. class iii. 2. 1. 8. " The debility of the exertion of voluntary efforts prevents the accomplishment of all the

great

great purposes of life. This often originates from a mistaken education; in which pleasure or vanity is made the immediate motive of action, and not future advantage, or what is term'd duty. This observation is of great value to those, who attend to the early education of their own children."

" I have seen one or two young married ladies of fortune, who perpetually became uneasy, and believed themselves ill, a week after their arrival in the country; and continued so uniformly during their stay; yet on their return to London or to Bath immediately lost all their complaints; and this I observed to happen to them repeatedly. All which I was led to ascribe to their being in their infancy surrounded with menial attendants, who had flattered them into the exertions, which they then used. And that in their mature years they became torpid for the want of this stimulus, and could not amuse themselves by any voluntary employment, but required ever after to be flattered into activity; or to be amused by others."

6. Rewards have been given to children to excite their industry in the performance of particular tasks; these are certainly less eligible motives to action than the fear of disgrace, the love of reputation, and above all the obligations of duty. Where never-

theless these are thought proper, the kind of rewards requires some attention; which should consist of books, or maps, or boxes of colours, or needle cases; but not of money, or of trinkets for ornamental dress, or of a glass of wine. Where money is given as a reward for industry in children, it may seem to them to be the proper motive of their actions instead of reputation or of duty; and may thus induce the vice of avarice or of extravagance. Where a fine cap or gown is given as a reward of diligence, the pride of dress may be produced, and become their great motive of action, instead of the love of reputation, or of duty. And lastly, where a glass of wine is given as a reward for industry, a child is taught to believe wine to be a most valuable acquisition, and a perpetual desire of it even to intoxication may be the consequence. I remember a wealthy farmer, who had two drunken sons, tho' he was a sober man himself, who told me, that he ascribed this great misfortune to his having occasionally given them in their early life a cup of ale as a reward for their exertions.—See Locke on education, sect. 52, &c.

7. A very accurate observer, who has long had the conduct of schools of various kinds for the instruction of the youth of both sexes, acquaints me, " That he has often with extreme surprize observed a child make a greater progress in some one branch

branch of education in three months, than another of similar age, opportunity, capacity, and even apparently of equal application, has been able to effect in three years." The same observation has been made by others, but he adds, " That this might probably arise from some trivial circumstance, which determined the inclination of the fortunate student; and that it is possible, that the means may sometime be discover'd of governing these incidents, and thus producing a new era in the art of education!"

Similar to this it has often been observed, that the first impressions made on our infant minds by accidental disgust, admiration, or flattery, are the frequent causes of our antipathies or aversions, and continue through life to bias our affections or mislead our judgments. One of my acquaintance can trace the origin of many of his own energies of action from some such remote sources; which justifies the observation of M. Rousseau, that the seeds of future virtues or vices are oftener sown by the mother than by the tutor.

Section XXXI.

LISPING.

LISPING is a defect of pronunciation occasion'd by children's making use of the sound of the letter TH sibilant instead of the letter S; as instead of "is it so," they say "ith it tho." To break this habit they must be taught to pronounce the S, by putting the point of the tongue against the roots of the upper teeth; and not to put it between their teeth as in pronouncing the TH. This is easily accomplish'd by putting their own finger against the point of the tongue, as it comes between their teeth, in attempting to pronounce the letter S, and pushing it back into the mouth.

I once saw a young lady, who after she had left school, had the habit of using occasionally, tho' not constantly, the guttural CH instead of the letter S, which was uncommonly disagreeable to english ears. She corrected this ill habit by being taught, as above,

above, how to place the tongue in pronouncing the S, but not without many trials and much attention for some weeks; as great efforts and pertinacious industry are required to break any habit, which has been long established.

Many children from the difficulty of speaking it are liable to a defective pronunciation of the letter R; this is indeed almost general in some parts of Northumberland, and is said to be a sound unknown in China; which obliged the catholic missionaries sent thither by Louis the 14th to change the name of the virgin Mary, from Maria into Malia, or from Mary into Mally. In speaking the letter R the middle of the tongue is made to vibrate with semivocal air; whereas in pronouncing L, the edges of the tongue only vibrate; the Northumberland vernacular R is form'd with sibilant air instead of semivocal air, or differs from the true R, as S differs from Z. Both which should be explain'd to those children, who have this imperfect pronunciation.

Among the lower orders of the people of London, who are called Cockneys, the letter W is pronounced sibilant like the German W, and not semivocal like our vernacular one; this seems to resemble the sound of V to inattentive ears; and these Cockneys, are thence supposed to use V instead of W, as Vomen and

and Vine, instead of Women and Wine. This defect is readily conquer'd by teaching such children to give more vocal sound to their W, by sounding it at first like OO.

Section XXXII.

STAMMERING.

THIS impediment of speech has generally for its remote cause a too great diffidence, or bashfulness, join'd with an ambition of shining in conversation; and for its immediate cause an interruption of the association of the initial letter of a word with the remainder of it. Which association is dissever'd by the ill-introduced sensation of awe, bashfulness, desire of shining, or fear of not succeeding; and then violent voluntary efforts are in vain employ'd to re-join the broken association, and give rise to various distortions of countenance, as explain'd in Zoonomia, vol. II. class iv. 2. 3. 1.

That this impediment of pronunciation is altogether a disease of the mind, and not of the organs of speech, is shewn by the stammerer being able to speak all words with perfect facility, when alone, as in repeating a play; but begins to hesitate, if any one approaches; or even if he imagines, that he is listen'd to. Those words also are most difficult to him to pronounce, which he is conscious, he cannot change for others, as when he is asked his own name, or the names of other persons, or of places; and the more so if he is aware, that the hearer is impatient to be inform'd, and that he cannot conjecture the name, before it is spoken.

It requires great attention, and much time to overcome this bad habit; they should be daily exercised in speaking single words as in spelling; and when they hesitate or find difficulty in announcing the beginning of a word, they should repeat it frequently aloud without the initial letter, and at length repeat it with the initial letter in a softer tone.

Suppose the stammerer finds difficulty in speaking the word " Paper," and says p, p, p, p, repeatedly, but cannot join the a after it. He must be taught to pronounce aper, aper, aper, without the initial p, for many successive times; and this aper should be spoken aloud with more breath than common, as if an h preceded it; and at length he should add in a softer tone the letter p to it.

This, together with an hourly attention to speaking and reading slowly, and practising in this manner every word, which is not readily spoken, both in private and in company, I am inform'd is the principle, on which those masters cure this impediment, who make it a profession; and to this should be added a frequent introduction to the society of strangers, in order to acquire less agitation or anxiety about the opinions of others.

Section XXXIII.

SQUINTING.

THIS defect of vision, which is term'd strabismns, may frequently be conquer'd in children, if it be attended to early, before it has been long establish'd by habit. In this deformity it generally happens, that one eye is better than the other, which induces the child to view objects with the best eye, and to hide the center of the other behind the nose. This greater inirritability of one eye is often occasion'd, I suspect, in infancy, by tying a bandage for too long a time over an eye, which has happen'd to be slightly inflamed, and thus decreasing it's power of action by disuse; in the same manner the large muscles of the body become weaken'd by long inaction; and the right arm is generally stronger than the left from it's having been more frequently exercised.

In this case if the best eye be for an hour or two, or longer, cover'd every day with gauze stretch'd upon a circular piece of whale-bone, so as to render the vision of this eye as indistinct as that of the other, the child will naturally turn them both to the same object, and in a little time the weak eye will become stronger by being used, or the strong one weaker by disuse, and the child will cease to squint.

Another kind of squinting is owing intirely to a bad habit, and consists in looking at objects with one eye only at a time. The owl bends both his eyes upon the object, which he observes; and by thus perpetually turning his head to the thing he inspects, appears to have greater attention to it; and has thence acquired the name of the bird of wisdom. All other birds, I believe, look at objects with one eye only, but it is with the eye nearest the object attended to; whereas in this kind of strabismus the person attends to objects with the most distant eye only. This habit has probably been produced, by a cap worn in infancy, which projected forward beyond the head on each side, like the blufts of a coach-horse, so as to make it easier for the child, as he lay in his cradle, to view oblique objects with the eye most distant from them; which kind of cap is therefore to be avoided.

A curious case of this ill habit of vision is related in the Philos. Transact. vol. 68. by Dr. Darwin; which was relieved by fixing a parchment gnomon on the nose of the little boy, which projected about an inch from the ridge of it, and caused him for a time to view oblique objects with that eye, which was nearest them.

Section XXXIV.

INVOLUNTARY MOTIONS.

BY confinement in a school-room for many successive hours, and that without being suffer'd to vary their posture, some of the more active and lively children are liable to gain tricks of involuntary actions, as twitchings of the face, restless gesticulations of the limbs, biting their nails, &c. which are generally at first occasion'd by the want of sufficient bodily exercise to expend the superfluous animal power, like the jumping of a squirrel in a cage; but are also liable to be caught by imitation of each other.

To prevent this kind of deformity children should be suffered to change their attitudes and situations more frequently; or to walk about, as they get their lessons. To counteract it the earliest attention is necessary; as a few weeks frequently establish a bad habit, which cannot be removed without great difficulty: This however may be effected early in the disease by a bandage nicely applied on the moving muscles, or by adhesive plasters put tightly over them; or by an issue placed over them, so as to give a little pain, when the muscles are thrown into action under it.

Section XXXV.

SWELL'D FINGERS,

AND kibed heels, are inflammations liable to affect tender children in many schools during the winter months. The latter of these complaints is generally owing to the coldness of a brick or plaster floor to their feet, or to their sitting in unchanged shoes and stockings, after walking in the wet; and the former to their being kept too long from the fire in the cold parts of the school-room without gloves.

Nothing prevents or cures these maladies but a due attention to keep the extremities of delicate children warm, either by clothing, exercise, or fire. The inflammation of the heels or toes may be sometimes removed by covering them with a double linen rag moistened in a saturnine solution made by dissolving half an ounce of sugar of lead in half a pint of water, to be renew'd morning and night. As the swelling of the fingers thus produced is liable to continue, and to injure the shape of them, it becomes of greater importance; but may in some measure be afterwards diminish'd or removed by the frequent application of vitriolic Ether to them.

The skin of the lips, and of the hands and arms of children is liable to become inflamed, and chopp'd, or rough, in frosty weather, owing both to the coldness and dryness of the air. The former is relieved by the application of a lip-salve made by mixing minium or red lead with spermaceti and oil to a proper consistance; or by blue mercurial ointment. The latter by wearing

leathern

leathern gloves, the inside of which is smear'd with spermaceti soften'd with a little oil, or with pomatum; gloves thus prepared prevent too great exhalation from the skin in frosty air, and the consequent too great dryness and roughness of it.

Section XXXVI.

BEDS.

THE rheumatism, and other inflammatory diseases, are frequently occasion'd in crowded schools by placing some of the beds with one side against a wall; where the weaker child confined by a stronger bedfellow is liable to lie for hours together with some part of it in contact with the cold wall; which in the winter months has often been attended with fatal consequences; and especially in those boarding schools, where the beds are small, and but one blanket allow'd to each of them, and a scanty feather-bed.

We are indued with a very accurate sense to distinguish heat and cold, which should be nicely attended to; as the extremes of

both

both of them are injurious to our health, and more so in our sleeping than in our waking hours. The extreme of heat is not much experienced in this climate, except when it is artificially produced; but that of cold is the cause of numerous diseases of the most fatal tendency. A severe continued frost may be borne by the strong, who can keep themselves warm by their activity, but is destructive to the weak and sedentary. In the year 1795 the weather in January, and in one week of February was uncommonly severe; the same five weeks in January and February 1796 were uncommonly mild; and it appears by the bills of mortality in London, that 2823 people died in these five weeks of frost in 1795; and that only 1471 died in the same five weeks of mild weather in 1796, which is not much more than half the number.—See a paper by Dr. Heberden in Philos. Transact. for the year 1796.

Some misinform'd parents have conceived, that a hard bed contributes to harden their children in respect to their bearing cold, and have on that account laid them on straw-mattresses, or on beds with boarded bottoms. The only difference between lying on a soft or hard bed consists in this; the weight of the body in the former case presses on a larger surface, and in the latter on a less; neither of which has any reference to the habits of tenderness or hardi-

hardiness in respect to cold and heat; unless indeed a feather-bed is so soft, that, as the child sinks down in the middle of it, the rising edges bend over him, and in part cover him. Perhaps beds made of soft leather properly prepared, and inflated with air, as the Emperor of Germany was said to use in camp, might be preferable on this account to feather-beds.

The beds for young children cannot therefore be too soft, however they may contribute to the indolence of grown people, provided they do not keep them too warm by bending over them as above described. But the too great hardness of beds is, I believe, frequently injurious to the shape of infants by occasioning them to rest on too few parts at a time; which hardens those parts by pressure, and prevents their proportionate growth. It also occasions their sleep to be less sound by the uneasiness it causes, and in consequence less refreshing.

The feet and knees and hands of weaker children are liable to become cold in bed in winter, on which account it is more salutary for them to sleep with a bed-fellow, rather than alone; as they then naturally put their cold knees or hands to their companion in bed, and thus frequently prevent rheumatic, and other inflammatory diseases of fatal event. For the same reason it is better for a new-born infant to sleep with it's mother in winter, or with a young nurse, than in a solitary crib by her bed-side; unless the artificial warmth of the room be more nicely graduated, than is commonly done.

For the same reason, where children are too feeble from illness, a fire should be allow'd in their bed-chamber in cold weather; as the cold air is otherwise injurious to their lungs, which cannot be clothed so as to prevent the contact of the air, like the other parts of the body; a fire contributes also to ventilate a room, and to circulate the air in it, and thence to render it more salutary; but it should not warm it to more than 60 or 65 degrees, that it's temperature may not differ too much from that of the external atmosphere; as those, who are kept generally too warm, are liable to take cold at every blast of air, not from the degree of cold, to which they happen to be exposed, but to it's difference from that, which they have been accustomed to.—See sect. xxvi.

The universal analogy derived from other animals, which produce a feeble offspring, evinces the truth of this doctrine, both in respect to the softness, and the due degree of warmth of their beds: Birds line the nests for their young with feathers; the eider duck, and the rabbit, pluck the down from their own

breasts

breasts to increase the softness of the beds for their tender offspring; and brood them with their wings, or clasp them to their bosoms for the sake of warmth.

The number of hours required for salutary sleep is greater for younger children, than for those more advanced; as during our progress through life we acquire greater facility in using our voluntary power, and recruit it in less time when exhausted. The younger classes of scholars may go to rest at seven, or eight; but the elder should be allow'd another hour for the purposes of reading or other kinds of improvement; the hour of rising must vary with the season.

Section XXXVII.

DIET.

MILK is the food designed by nature for young animals, and should be given them in it's recent state. As the cream is the most nourishing part of the milk, and is easier of digestion than the coagulable or cheesy part; and as milk constitutes a principal portion of the aliment of children; to take off the cream once, or even twice, as is practised in some boarding schools, before it is given to the children, is a shameful circumstance of parsimony, and very injurious to their healths.—See sect. xxx, on punishments.

Nor should the milk given to children be long kept in a boiling heat; because much of it's fragrant oil is then evaporated, as is evident from the fine odour of the steam of it, when taken from the fire; and it's further deterioration from long boiling is shewn by it's then inducing constipation, which is contrary to it's effect in it's recent and natural state.

Nevertheless even new milk does not always agree with children, after they have pass'd the years of infancy. For milk taken into the stomach must be always previously curdled or coagulated, before it can be digested, or converted into nourishment: Hence milk is always found curdled in the stomachs of calves, and the acid juice of their stomachs is used to coagulate the milk in the process of cheese-making: Now the stomachs of young children abound more with this acid juice than in their riper years, and when a sufficient quantity of it is not produced for the purpose of curdling the milk, which they drink, it is liable to disagree.

To

To these few therefore, whose stomachs do not easily digest the coagulable part of milk, other fluid food should be allow'd to breakfast, as gruel, or tea with cream and sugar in it, and with bread and butter; and to supper, a slice of cold meat, or of cheese, or tart, or bread and butter, with small beer or water for drink; but it is probable, that milk might be made to agree with all stomachs, if it was previously curdled by rennet, as I have often recommended with success to elderly persons; or by letting it stand, till it becomes spontaneously sour like buttermilk, as is the custom of the inferior people of Scotland; except nevertheless where the distaste of the child is owing to prejudice or caprice, which is then incurable but by time.

For dinner animal food plain dress'd, with vegetables or bread, and pudding of wheat flour, milk, and eggs, with sugar or butter, are more nourishing than vegetable sustenance alone. Wheat flour contains more nutriment than that of rice, or barley, or oats; as it possesses more starch in proportion to it's bulk, and a gluten approaching to animal matter. But much salt or spice should not be allow'd in the diet of children, as they are certainly unwholesome by inducing a weakness of the capillary and absorbent systems of vessels in consequence of their too great stimulus, and contain no nourishment.

As butter and sugar are perhaps the most nutritive of animal and vegetable substances, they may be more easily taken to excess; on which account some mistaken parents have totally prohibited the use of them; which is a great disadvantage to weaker children, who require more nutritive diet in less bulk than stronger ones.

For the drink of the more robust children water is preferable, and for the weaker ones, small beer; but in this, as well as in the choice of solid food, their palates should be consulted; for the nice discernment of this sense is bestow'd on us by nature to distinguish, what the stomach can best digest. It should however be observed, that in artificial viands the taste cannot distinguish, what is unwholesome; as sugar may be mix'd with arsenic. So in the drinking of fermented liquors, as ale or wine, which are chemical productions, the palate is not to be consulted; a glass of meer wine should never be given to children, as it injures their tender stomachs like a glass of brandy or rum or gin to a grown person; and induces those diseases, which it is often erroneously given to prevent; as weakness of digestion, with the production of worms in consequence. Wine nevertheless diluted with thrice it's quantity of water may be allow'd, if required, instead of small beer; or ale or cider diluted with thrice their quantities of water.

Ripe

Ripe fruits, or fruit pies, are peculiarly ferviceable to the conftitutions of children, as well as agreeable to their palates; as they are known to prevent biliary concretions, and confequent jaundice; and on the fame account to render the fkin clearer and fairer, as well as to counteract the tendency to putrid difeafes. Thefe fhould therefore be allow'd to children at all feafons; and may either occafionally conftitute a part of their diet; or may be recommended to them, when they lay out part of their pocket-money with huckfters, in preference to feed-cakes, gingerbread, or fugar-plumbs; the former of which are generally made of bad flour deteriorated by fpice; and the latter are liable to be colour'd with gamboge, vermillion, verdigreafe, or other noxious drugs.

Too long fafting, or food of lefs nourifhment than they have been accuftomed to, are peculiarly injurious to children; as they weaken their power of digeftion, impair their ftrength, and impede their growth. The children of the inferior poor, and of families, which have adopted fome ill-advifed rules of abftemious diet, are frequently ftarved into the fcrophula, and become pale-faced and bloated, owing to deficiency of the quantity of blood, and to want of fufficient ftimulus to the abforbent fyftem.

If young people are thought to be too corpulent, a diminution
of

of food with an increase of exercise, when they have obtain'd their full growth, may be used with advantage; but even then not without caution. Since young ladies, after they have left school, who by ill advice use too great abstinence, are liable to become pale and emaciated, and to fall into universal debility; which remains through a diseased and comfortless life.

Section XXXVIII.

ECONOMY.

1. A Due regard to the prudent expenditure of their money, a proper care of their clothes, and a parsimonious attention to the lapse of time, should be inculcated into the minds of young ladies. To effect these purposes one efficacious method, where the usual exhortations fail, may be to suffer their imprudence to produce some inconvenience to themselves; which they should be permitted to feel to a proper degree.

Thus a profuse unnecessary expenditure of their pocket money will shortly induce poverty; which should by no means be alleviated

viated by a fresh supply of money; till the inconvenience produced has effected a conviction of the impropriety of their conduct. Except when the expenditure has been made for some laudable purpose, and then no time should be lost in restoring the power of repeating it.

The same means may be used in respect to their omission to take care of their clothes; they should find the necessity of repairing them with their own hands, or of foregoing some visiting amusements, till new ones can be procured; that thus the consequent inconvenience may teach them economy, if they are otherwise too inattentive to the usual admonitions on these subjects.

In respect to the economy of time the hours of amusement and of exercise should be regularly counted; and the length of time young ladies employ in dressing should be nicely attended to; as in adult life the hours consumed at the toilet of some ladies is perfectly ridiculous, and detains them from more important duties. Perhaps a stated time might be allow'd the young ladies for adjusting the articles of their dress, that they might acquire a habit of disposing them with neatness, taste, and elegance, and yet with expedition.

2. Men

2. Men are generally train'd from their early years to the business or profession, in which they are afterwards to engage; but it most frequently happens to ladies, that tho' destined to the superintendance of a future family, they receive scarcely any previous instruction; but begin this important office with a profound ignorance of the value of money, and of the proper application of the things, which surround them.

Many young ladies destitute of mothers, and without a home, are continued at school to a later age; such should be form'd into a class, and properly instructed in domestic economy; each of them superintending the business of the family, a week or a month by turns; not only providing for the table, and directing the cookery, but they should also be taught other parts of domestic employment, as cutting out linens, and making them up with plain and strong needle-work, either for their own families, or to be given as clothing for necessitous infants or mothers.

Such an addition of domestic knowledge and benevolent industry to ornamental accomplishments would give the school, that procures it, a decided advantage over other schools, which have no such institution.

Section XXXIX.

SCHOOL-EDUCATION.

THE advantages of a school-education, where twenty or thirty children are properly instructed, over that in a private family are derived from several sources. First, it must be observed, that almost all our exertions in early life are owing to our imitating others; in childhood we are most liable to imitate the actions of those, who are somewhat older than ourselves; and in manhood, of those we are in somewhat higher life; whence the general prevalence of fashion in dress and manners. Now there are more examples to cause this imitative activity in well conducted schools, and the children in consequence become more active in the pursuit of their studies, and in the acquirement of their accomplishments.

It may be added, that not only children, before they have acquired the use of reason, or voluntary deliberation, but that the greatest part of adult mankind learn all the common arts of life by imitating

tating others; and that even dumb creatures seem capable of acquiring knowledge with greater facility by imitating each other, than by any methods, by which we can teach them. Thus dogs, when they are sick, learn of each other to eat grass as an emetic; and cats to moisten their paws for the purpose of washing their faces. And the readiest way to instruct all brute animals is by practising them with others of the same species; which have already learnt the arts, we wish them to acquire, as explain'd in Zoonomia, vol. I. sect. 22. 3.

A second advantage of schools, when well conducted, is, that children often take pleasure in teaching each other, insomuch that at boy's schools I have often observed, that the lower classes have learnt more from their school-fellows of the higher classes, than even from their masters; which has sometimes arisen from the friendship, or vanity of the elder boy, and sometimes from the solicitation of the lower one; but has in all cases been advantageous to both of them.

A third superiority of school-education arises from an emulation, which naturally exists, where many pursue the same studies, but which should not be encouraged by rewards or degradations; as it then may degenerate into envy or hatred; but should in general

neral be left intirely to it's own operation; as mention'd in sect. xxx.

A fourth advantage of school-education is from the children acquiring a kind of practical physiognomy; which renders them more intelligent, and more interesting companions; and is of greater consequence in our passage through life, than almost any single accomplishment, as explain'd in sect. vi. and sect. xxiv. of this work.

Fifthly, where languages are learnt by conversation, as is generally practised in teaching the french language, a school-education properly conducted is much superior to that of a governess in a private family. And languages are so much easier taught to children by conversation than by the abstract rules of grammar, that Mr. Locke is solicitous to have the latin and greek languages taught by conversation in boys' schools; and thinks the time of learning words might thus be much shorten'd, which now occupies seven or eight years; part of which might be much better employ'd in acquiring the knowledge of things.

The Philosopher, who despising the goods of fortune said, " he was rich, though he carried about with him every thing, which he possess'd," meant to assert, that strength of mind join'd with strength of body, were superior to any other advantages of life. A good education furnishes us with this inestimable treasure; it accompanies us at home, travels with us abroad; delights us in solitude, graces us in society; comforts us in misfortune, guards us in prosperity; contributes to the happiness of others, and ensures our own.

Section XL.

CATALOGUE OF BOOKS.

I Beg leave to apprize the reader, that I have inserted a great part of the following catalogue of books for the younger children, because they were recommended to me by ladies, whose opinions I had reason to regard, and not from my own attentive perusal of them; which has been prevented by my other necessary occupations. Such of them therefore, as are less generally known, a parent or governess will please to read, before they put them

them into the hands of their children. And I can only add, that if I had myself been better acqainted with them, the collection would probably have been lefs numerous.

LEARNING TO READ.—SECT. 3.

Spelling-Book, by D. Fenning. 1s.
Harry and Lucy. Cadell, London.
Mrs. Barbauld's Spelling-Books.
Mrs. Barbauld's Leffons. 2s.
Fabulous Hiftory of Robins, by Mrs. Trimmer.
Fairy Spectator. 1s. Marfhall.
Circuit of Human Life. Marfhall. 1s.
Scenes for Children. Marfhall. 1s.
Rational Sports. Marfhall. 1s.
Rational Dame. Marfhall. 1s. 6d.
Hiftory of England, with cuts. 1 vol. Power. 1s.
Looking Glafs for the Mind, with cuts by Bewick. 3s. 6d.
Cobwebs to catch Flies. 2 vols. Marfhall. 2s.
Little Truths. 2 vols.———Little Mentor.
Blind Child. 2s.———Poor Child's Friend.
Davenport Family.———Letitia Lively.
Village School. 2 vols. Marfhall. 1s.
Prince Le Boo. 1s. 6d.
Sandford and Merton. 3 vols. Stockdale. 10s. 6d.
Parent's Affiftant. 3 vols. Johnfon. 4s. 6d.
Evenings at Home. 6 vols. Johnfon. 9s.
Leifure Hours, by P. Wakefield. 2 vols. 3s.
Mental Improvement, by P. Wakefield. 2 vols. 3s.
Juvenile Anecdotes. 1s. 6d.
Pleafing Inftructor. 2 vols. 3s. each.
Rudiments of Reafon. 3 vols. 4s. 6d.
Rural Walks, by Ch. Smith. 2 vols. Cadell. 5s.
Rambles farther, by Ch. Smith. 2 vols. Cadell. 5s.
Juvenile Magazine. Marfhall. 3s. 6d.
Governefs of an Academy. Rivington.

Progress of Man and Society, by Trusler. 1 vol. small.
Beauties of the Creation, by Riley.——Mentoria, by Ann Murry, 3s. 6d.
Gay's Fables.——Dodsley's Esop's Fables.

There are innumerable other books publish'd for the use of children from one penny to a shilling and upwards by almost every bookseller in London. Many of the above are the works of reputable writers; and the others have been recommended to me by those, who have perused them.

GRAMMAR. SECT. 5.

Grammatical Introduction. Gales, Sheffield.
Mrs. Devis's Rudiments of Grammar. 1s. 6d.
Lowth's Introduction to English Grammar. Dodsley. 1s. 6d.
Ash's Grammar. 1s.——Smetham's practical Grammar. 1s. 6d.
Johnson's English Dictionary. Oct. edit. 8s.——Entick's Spelling Dictionary. 2s.
General Grammar, by Messrs. Port Royal.
Took's Epea Pteroenta, or Diversions of Purley.
Jeu de Grammaire, par de Gaultier. 1l. 1s.

These three last treat of Grammar too minutely and artificially, rather as a science itself, than as an aid to facilitate the acquirement of languages, and are therefore less adapted to schools.

FRENCH LANGUAGE. SECT. 6.

Chambaud's Grammar and Vocabulary. 3s. 6d. and 2s. 6d.
Cours de Lectures pour Les Enfans, par Abbe Gaultier.
La Bagatelle. 2 vols. Marshall.——Petites Miscel. pour les Enfans.
Le Magazin des Enfans, par M. de Beaumont. 6s.
Education complete, par M. de Beaumont.
Instruction pour les Jeunes Dames.
Theatre d'Education, par M^{de} de Genlis.—Les Veillies du Chateau, par M^{de} de Genlis.
L'Ami des Enfans, par Berquin.——L'Ami des Adolescents, par Berquin.
Mythologie des Jeunes Demoiselles, par M. de la Mimardiere, 2 vs. 12mo. fr. & eng.
Conversations d'Emilie, french & english.
Lodoick, french & english, 6 vols. 15s.——Idylles de Gesner.
Oevres de Florian.——Les Petites Montagnards.
La Campagne de la Jeunesse.——Varietes Historique.
L'Eleve et son Instructrice.——Drames et Dialogues de Mad. de la Fite.
Questions par Mad. de la Fite.——— Fables de Cambray.
Lettres de Mad. de Lambert a son fils.
Discours sur l'Histoire universal, par Bossuet.

Gil

Gil Blas.———Paul et Virginie, par St. Pierre.
Lettres d' une Peruvienne.———Lettres de Sevigné.
Voyages de Cyrus. Numa Pompilius. Telemaque. 3s. 6d.
Voyages de Jeune Anacharis. 6 vols. 12mo.

ITALIAN LANGUAGE.   SECT. 6.

Tasso.———Metastasio.———Select Plays of Goldoni.—Scelta Italiane, 3s. 6d. Johnson
A Selection of Metastasio's Works, in 2 vols. small. Payne.
Ganganelli.———Bentivoglio.———Pastor Fido.———Gil Blas, translated into Italian.
Lettres d' une Peruvienne, translated into Italian, with accents.
Telemaco, a translation from Telemaque.———Baretti's Italian Grammar.
Baretti's Italian Dictionary, 1l. 10s.———Baretti's Italian Library, 1 vol. 8vo.

The greatest part of these french and italian books for the use of children, as well as very many english ones, may be had at Mr. Peacocks's juvenile library, Oxford street, London.

ARITHMETIC.   SECT. 7.

Vise's Tutor's Guide, 3s.———Hutton's practical Arithmetic, 2s. 6d.
Wingate's Arithmetic, 4s.———Walkingame's Tutor's Assistant, 2s.

GEOGRAPHY.   SECT. 8.

Large well-colour'd four sheet Maps of the World, of Europe, Asia, Africa, and America, and of England.
Geographical Cards by Newberry, 2s. 6d.———Geographical Cards by Bowles, 2s. 6d.
Geographical Cards with prints of dresses.———Fairman's Geography, 8vo. 5s.
Turner's Geography, 12mo. 3s. 6d.———Faden's Maps with blank outlines, 7s. 6d.
Moral System of Geography, 12mo. Riley———Harris on the Globes, 4s.
Guthrie's Geographical Grammar, 10s. 6d.———Brooke's Gazetteer, 8s.
Abbe Gualtier's jeu de Geography, 1l. 11s. 6d.

CIVIL HISTORY.   SECT. 9.

History of England, with prints. 1s. Power.
Characters of Kings of England, with heads by Bewick, 1 vol. Newberry.
Trimmer's Histories of England, Greece, and Rome.
Riley's historical pocket Library, 6 vols. 12mo.———Rollins's Ancient History.
Goldsmith's Histories of Greece, Rome, England, and Scotland.
Millot's Elements of History.———Plutarch's Lives.
Priestley's Lectures on History.———Priestley's Chart of History, 10s. 6d.
Priestley's Chart of Biography, 10s. 6d.———Mrs. Chapone's Letter on Chronology.

Circle of Sciences, by Newberry, the 7th vol. on Chronology.
Voyages and Travels, by Mavor. Newberry. Now publishing in No. 12mo. 1797.
Beauties of England ———— Beauties of Nature and Art, 13 vols. 12mo. Payne. 1743.

Hume's and Henry's Histories of England; Robertson's Histories of Charles the 5th, and of America; with Rollin's and Millot's antient and modern Histories, are too voluminous for school books.

NATURAL HISTORY. SECT. 10.

Galton's Treatise on Birds, 3 vols. 12mo. Johnson.
Natural History of Beasts and of Birds, 2 vols. Newberry.
History of Quadrupeds, by Mrs. Teachwell, 2 vols. 5s. Marshall.
Rational Dame, 1s. 6d. Marshall.————Bewick's account of Quadrupedes, 14s.
Goldsmith's Animated Nature, 8 vols. 8vo. 2l.
Buffon's Natural History abridged, 2 vols. 8vo. 17s. Johnson.

Dictionaire Raisonnè, par Bomare, 6 vols. 8vo. is a very useful work on Natural History to be occasionally refer'd to, rather than to be read as a school-book. Pennant's books of Zoology; Barbut's Histoire des Insectes; White's Natural History of Selbourn; and many other works with numerous plates, are too voluminous or too expensive, for the use of schools.

RUDIMENTS OF TASTE. SECT. 11.

Spectator, vol. 6, No. 411, to 422.————Burke on Sublime and Beautiful. 5s.
Blair's Lectures.————Hogarth's Analysis of Beauty, 10s. 6d.
Akenside's Pleasures of Imagination, 8vo. 3s.
Longinus on the Sublime, translated by Smith.
Mason's English Garden.————Wheatly on ornamental Gardening.
Price's Essay on Picturesque.————Gilpin's Picturesque Views.
Sir Joshua Reynolds's Discourses to the Academy.————Clio on Taste, 3s.
Beauties of Shakespear, 3s. 6d. Kearsley.————Of Pope, 2 vols. 7s.————Of Johnson, 3s. 6d.————Of Rambler, Adventurer, &c. 2 vols. 7s.————Of Sterne, 3s. 6d.————Of Spectator, Tatler, &c. 2 vols. 6s.
Warton's History of Poetry.————Pope's Essay on Criticism.
Addison's Criticisms on Milton in the Spectator.
Spence's Criticism on Pope's Odyssy.————Mrs. Montague's Essay on Shakespear.
Warton's Essay on Pope, 2 vols. 8vo.
Lord Kaim's Elements of Criticism, 2 vols. 14s.

This last work is highly ingenious, but too abstruse for young ladies, who might more easily improve their taste in respect to visible objects by frequently being shewn with proper remarks a select collection of the prints of beautiful landscapes, or of beautiful figures.
HEATHEN

HEATHEN MYTHOLOGY. SECT. 13.

Young Ladies Mythology, my Mifs de la Mimardiere, 2 vols. 12mo.
Bell's Pantheon, 4to. 1l. 1s. ——The notes in Pope's tranflation of Homer.
Dannet's Dictionary, in french or englifh, 4to.
Inftruction fur le Metamorphofes d' Ovide, par M. Ragois.
Garth's Tranflation of Ovid's Metamorphofes.
Spence's Polymetis, folio. 1l. 1s.——Bryant's Mythology, 3 vols. 4to. 3l. 15s.
Abbe de Pluche's Hiftory of the Heavens, 2 vols. 8vo.

Thefe three laft works are too difficult or too voluminous for young ladies, who might learn heathen mythology more eafily and more agreeably from a felect collection of the impreffions from antique gems and medallions, or of prints of antient ftatues.

DISSERTATIONS. SECT. 14.

Spectator, 8 vols. 1l.——Guardian, 2 vols.——Tatler. 6 vols. 1l. 10s.
The World, 4 vols. 14s.——Rambler, 4 vols. 12s.——Adventurer, 4 vols. 12s.
Mirror, 3 vols. 9s.——Anacharfis, tranflated from the french, 6 vols. 8vo.
Converfations of Emelia, 2 vols. 7s. Marfhall.——Turkifh Spy.
Effays for young Ladies, by Mifs H. Moore.
Improvement of the Mind, by Mrs. Chapone, 2s.
Lambert's Advice to a Son and Daughter.
Gregory's Advice to a Daughter, 3s.——Locke on Education, 3s.
Mifs Bowdler's Works, 2 vols. 8vo. 8s.——Mifs Talbot's Works, 2 vols.
Calender of Nature, by Dr. Akin, 1s.
Introduction to the Knowledge of Nature.
Hallifax's Advice to a Daughter.——Fitzofborn's Letters, 6s.
Con Phillips's Whole Duty of Woman.
Lord Chefterfield's Letters; the 1ft volume only. 4 vols. 8vo.
Some of Lady W. Montague's Letters, 2 vols. 6s.
Rollin's Belles Lettres, 4 vols. 12mo. 12s.
Britifh Plutarch.——Johnfon's Lives of the Poets.
Aikin's Life of Howard.——Keir's Life of Day.
Franklin's Life, by himfelf.——Enfield's Speaker.
Elegant Extracts, 3 vols. large octavo.——Preceptor, 2 vols. 14s.

The englifh and french profe tranflations of fome of the antient claffics fhould be added, as Mrs. Carter's Epictetus; Mrs. Fielding's Xenophon; Melmouth's Epiftles of Pliny, and of Cicero to his Friends; and the Abbé Mongault's of thofe to Atticus; and many others.

PLAYS. SECT. 14.

Addison's Cato.——Thomson's Tragedies.
Caractacus and Elfrida, by Mr. Mason.——Edgar and Elfrida.
Cumberland's Comedies.——Sheridan's Comedies.——Beauties of Shakespear.
Sacred Dramas, by Miss Moore.——Sacred Dramas, by Mad. de Genlis.
Sacred Dramas, by Metastasio.——L'Ami des Enfans.
Theatre of Education, by Mad. de Genlis.
Tragedies de Racine.——Tragedies de Corneille.

NOVELS. SECT. 14.

Sandford and Merton. 3 vols. Stockdale. 10s. 6d.
Children's Friend, by Berquin.——New Robinson Crusoe. 3s. 6d.
Adelard and Theodore, by Mad. de Genlis.
Tales of the Castle, by Mad. de Genlis, 5 vols. 10s. 6d.
Moral Tales, by Dr. Percival, 5s. Johnson.
Moral Tales, by Miss Mitchel, 2 vols. 8vo.
Stories from Life, by M. Wolstencroft, 2s. 6d. Johnson.
Rasselas, by Dr. Johnson, with Continuation.——Agatha, 1 vol. 12mo.
Plain Sense, 3 vols. 12mo. Lane.——Disobedience, 4 vols. 12mo. Lane.
Edward, by the Author of Zeluco.——Evelina, by Miss Burney, 2 vols. 7s.
Cecilia, by Miss Burney, 5 vols. 15s.——Camilla, by Miss Burney, 5 vols. 1l. 1s.
Emmeline and Ethelinda, by Ch. Smith.——Simple Story, by Mrs. Inchbald.
Emily Montague, by Miss Brooks.——Female Quixott, 2 vols. 6s.
Belisarius, by Marmontel, 3s. 6d.——Caroline de Leitchfield.
Les Romans de L'Abbè Prevot.——Laure, 5 vols. 12mo.

POEMS. SECT. 14.

Gay's Fables, 3s.——Thomson's Seasons, 2s. 6d.
Gisborne's Walks in a Forest.——Moore's Fables for the Female Sex, 5s.
Hayley's Serena, and his Epistles.——Cowper's Task.
Gray's Poems, 5s.——Collins' Poems, 3s.
Goldsmith's Poems, 2 vols. 7s.——Lord Lyttleton's Poems.
Addison's Poems.——Carter's Poems.
Aikin's Poems.——Jerningham's Poems.
Akenside's Pleasures of Imagination.
Mason's Works, 3 vols. 8vo.——Milton's Poetical Works.
Pope's translation of Homer's Iliad.
——————— of Homer's Odyssey.

Pope's Works,---Dr. Watson's edition.
Garth's translation of Ovid's Metamorphoses.
Dryden's, or Pitt's translation of Virgil.
Hoole's translation of Tasso's Jerusalem deliver'd, 2 vols. 14s.
Mickle's translation of Camoen's Lusiad.
Botanic Garden, 2 vols.
Dodsley's Collection of Poems.
Elegant Extracts, in verse.
Henriade de Voltaire.

ARTS AND SCIENCES. SECT. 15.

Lee's Introduction to Botany, 7s. 6d.
Botanical Dialogues, for the use of Schools, by M. E. Jackson. Johnson.
Families of Plants, translated from Linneus, 2 vols. 16s. Johnson.
System of Vegetables, from Linneus, 2 vols. 18s. Leigh.
Notes on vol. II. of Botanic Garden.
Curtis's Botanical Magazine, with colour'd prints; many volumes of which are already publish'd, and which continues to be now publish'd at one shilling a number, 1797.
Martyn's translation of Rousseau's Letters on Botany.
Lavoisier's Elements of Chymistry, 2 vols. 8vo.
Fourcroy's Philosophy of Chymistry, 2s.
Watson's Chymical Essays.
Kirwan's Mineralogy, 2 vols. 8vo. 12s.
Notes on Vol. I. of Botanic Garden.
Grey's Memoria Technica.
Gurney's Short-Hand, 10s. 6d.
Ladies' Encyclopedia, by Seally, 3 vols. 12mo. 15s. Murray.
Circle of Sciences, 7 vols. small, 7s. Newberry.
Introduction to Arts and Sciences, by Turner, 1 vol. Crowder.

MORALITY. SECT. 21.

Elements of Morality, translated from Salzmann, 3 vols. 10s. 6d.
Gisborne's Duties of the Female Sex, 6s.
Letters of Lady Russel, 8vo. 6s.

Economy of Human Life, 1s. 6d.
Old Whole Duty of Man.
Paley's System of Morality.
Gisborne's Answer to Paley.

These two last works are too scientific for young minds to encounter.

RELIGION. SECT. 22.

Select parts of Scripture.
Barbauld's Hymns, 1s.
Sacred Dramas, by Charl. Smith.
———————— by Mad. de Genlis.
———————— by Metastasio.
Old Whole Duty of Man, 3s.
Blair's Sermons, 4 vols. 1l. 6s.
Carr's Sermons.———Ogden's Sermons.
Baron Haller's Letter to his Daughter.
Lady Pennington's Advice to her Daughter.
Fashionable Religion, by Miss H. Moore.
Wisdom of God in the Creation, by Ray.
Durham's Physico-Theology.
Divine Benevolence asserted, by Dr. Balguy, 1s. 6d. Davis.
Trimmer's Sacred History, 6 vols. 18s.
Butler's Analysis.
Paley's Evidences of Christianity, 2 vols. 8vo.

Books of controversial divinity are not recommended to Ladies.

APOLOGY

APOLOGY FOR THE WORK.

THE foregoing treatise was written at the desire of Miss S. and Miss M. Parker; who were themselves educated for the purpose of educating others; and on that account were originally placed in different seminaries for female tuition; and afterwards engaged themselves for a time as teachers in other schools, and in private families; the better to qualify themselves for the arduous task of conducting a boarding school for the education of young ladies.

About four years ago a house was offer'd to sale at Ashborne in Derbyshire, at the very extremity of the town, in a most pleasant and healthy situation, on a dry sandy soil, with excellent water, well shelter'd from the north-east, and commanding an extensive prospect of Sir Brooke Boothby's park, and it's beautiful environs; through which are pleasant walks at all seasons of the year; and of which an engraved plate was presented to me by Sir Brooke Boothby as a frontispiece to this work.

A spacious walled garden adjoins the house, at the bottom of which is a stream of water, which may sometime be converted into a river-bath.

Miss PARKERS procured this eligible situation, and had the house well fitted up for the purposes of a boarding school. It consists of an ample school-room, and an ample dining-room, and four smaller parlours, on the principal floor; with two staircases, one of which is of stone. The whole is airy and well lighted; and now contains about thirty pupils without being crowded.

They next had the good fortune to engage very excellent teachers in dancing, music, and drawing, from Nottingham, Derby, and Lichfield, with a polite emigrant as French-master; and lastly applied to me for any ideas, I could furnish them with, on the subject of female education. And now, as their establishment has succeeded to their utmost wish, have expressed a desire, that I would give to the public, what I wrote originally for their private inspection.

I have only to add, that a copy of the manuscript has been seen by many of the ingenious of both sexes, and much improved by their observations; to whom I here beg leave to return my most grateful acknowledgments.

DERBY, January 1st, 1797.

THE TERMS OF MISS PARKERS SCHOOL,

At ASHBOURN in Derbyshire.

EMBROIDERY and Needle-work of all kinds both useful and ornamental, reading with propriety, grammar, a taste for english classics, an outline of history both ancient and modern, with geography and the use of the globes, are taught by Miss PARKERS; who carefully attend to the morals as well as to the manners of their pupils, and to their health as well as to their acquirements.

	£.	s.	d.
Board for the year,	18	18	0
Entrance,	2	2	0
Tea, if required, per quarter,	0	10	6
Washing, per quarter,	0	14	0
Geography, per quarter,	0	10	6
French, Music, Dancing, and Drawing, each per quarter,	1	1	0
Entrances,	1	1	0

It is expected that each young lady will give a quarter's notice previous to her leaving school, or pay a quarter's board. Each young lady is required to bring one pair of sheets, two towels, a knife and fork, and a silver spoon.

Books printed by the Author.

FAMILIES OF PLANTS, translated from the Genera Plantarum of Linneus, to which is prefix'd an alphabetical list of all the names of plants and other botanical words accented, to ascertain their pronunciation, 2 vols. 8vo. 16s. Johnson.

THE SYSTEM OF VEGETABLES, translated from the last edition of the Systema Vegetabilium of Linneus, 2 vols. 8vo. 18s. Leigh.

BOTANIC GARDEN, 2 vols. 4to. 1l. 13s.

ZOONOMIA, or the Laws of Organic Life, 2 vols. 4to. 2l. 16s. 6d.

THE END.